CW01189066

WEAPON

MEDIEVAL HANDGONNES

SEAN McLACHLAN

Series Editor Martin Pegler

First published in Great Britain in 2010 by Osprey Publishing,
PO Box 883, Oxford, OX1 9PL, UK
1385 Broadway, 5th Floor, New York, NY 10018, USA
Email: info@ospreypublishing.com

OSPREY is a trademark of Osprey Publishing, a division of Bloomsbury Publishing Plc

Transferred to digital print on demand 2017

First published 2010
1st impression 2010

Printed and bound in Great Britain

A CIP catalogue record for this book is available from the British Library.

Print ISBN: 978 1 84908 155 9
PDF eBook ISBN: 978 1 84908 156 6

Sean McLachlan has asserted his/her right under the Copyright, Designs and Patents Act, 1988, to be identified as the Author of this Work.

Page layout by Ben Salvesen
Battlescene artwork by Gerry and Sam Embleton
Index by Alan Thatcher
Typeset in Sabon and Univers
Originated by PDQ Digital Media Solutions

The Woodland Trust
Osprey Publishing is supporting the Woodland Trust, the UK's leading woodland conservation charity, by funding the dedication of trees.

MIX
Paper from responsible sources
FSC www.fsc.org FSC® C013604

Artist's note

Readers may care to note that the original paintings from which the colour plates in this book were prepared are available for private sale. All reproduction copyright whatsoever is retained by the Publishers. All enquiries should be addressed to:

www.gerryembleton.com

The Publishers regret that they can enter into no correspondence upon this matter.

Dedication

For Almudena, my wife, and Julián, my son.

Editor's note

Occasional references are made in this book to the pre-decimal British currency of pounds, shillings and pence. For those unfamiliar with the system, 12 old pence (12d) made one shilling (1s), and 20 shillings made one old pound (£1). The conversion to decimal currency was made on the basis of one shilling equalling five new pence, and with 100 new pence in the pound.

The following will help in converting other measurements between metric and imperial:

1 mile = 1.6km
1lb = 0.45kg
1 yard = 0.9m
1ft = 0.3m
1in = 25.4mm
100fps = 30.48m/s

Acknowledgements

My research on this subject was made possible through the advice and help of dozens of historians, archaeologists, museum curators, and re-enactors. I would especially like to thank historian Kelly DeVries for his insights into 14th- and 15th-century technology, Gerry Embleton for much useful material, Swiss re-enactor Ulrich Bretscher for his first-hand knowledge of firing early handgonnes, The Middelaldercentret in Denmark for information on their gunpowder experiments, and the Company of the Wolfe Argent for providing the excellent firing sequences found in this book. Special thanks go to Professor Bert Hall of the University of Toronto for enlightening me as to the uses of urine from a wine-drinking man.

Cover illustration from the Swiss Amtliche Berner Chronik of 1483, by Diebold Schilling. (Burgerbibliothek Bern, Mss.h.h.l.1, p.347). Handgonne photographs (top) courtesy Royal Armouries, and Danish National Museum of Military History.

Title page image used with permission of the British Library (Royal 14 E IV f.23)

CONTENTS

INTRODUCTION

This book covers the development of hand-held black powder weapons from their earliest beginnings in the mid-14th century through their development over the next 150 years. These simple weapons, lit by a slow match held in the hand for want of a trigger and lock, went through a rapid development and a variety of styles before being replaced by the matchlock *arquebus* in the late 15th and early 16th centuries.

Pre-matchlock handgonnes have been much maligned by historians, many of whom dismiss them as inaccurate, primitive contraptions that did little other than scare the enemy and endanger the user; however, an examination of medieval chronicles and the experiences of modern experimental archaeologists and re-enactors show otherwise. Early handgonnes, while slow to reload and inaccurate at long range, had superior penetrative power compared to bows and crossbows, and proved their worth time and again on the battlefield. The fact that they spread so quickly – within a century of their invention they were considered a vital part of every European army, and within another century they had started to displace the crossbow – shows they were a valuable addition to the arsenal of the medieval soldier.

OPPOSITE
A man firing a large handgonne of the socketed variety from Konrad Kyeser's *Bellifortis*, 1405. Unlike the other image reproduced from the same book (see page 29), this man is lighting his own weapon. He appears to use a bent piece of iron. While modern re-enactors have found that hot irons tend to bend because of the gonne's recoil, this one looks sufficiently thick to withstand it. (Niedersächsische Staats- und Universitätsbibliothek Göttingen)

It is not known exactly when hand-held black powder weapons were first used, nor when the handgonne was later replaced by the matchlock. Although the first matchlock arquebuses appeared as early as the first quarter of the 15th century, pre-matchlock handgonnes did not immediately disappear, and in some places continued to be used well into the 16th century. It is difficult to identify from some contemporary chronicles and images whether the firearms being illustrated have matchlocks or not. Artwork from even very late in the 15th century shows the matchlock had not come into universal use, and it may have been a minority elite weapon within a larger group of handgonnes. Thus some engagements, such as the battles of the Swiss–Burgundian Wars of the

Ignis pro sagittare volante R(ecipe) petrolei unc(i)a partem sulphuris vivi ii partes olei laterini seu benedicti unc(i)a partem intinge lanam id est bombace wolgauter bawmbol et pone in talem patellulam ferream reponendo in ore sagitte volat(ilis)

et in longo collo reponatur candela sulphuris ardens que incendet crucibulum vel patellam et veniet ignis currens ore inextinguibilis et ad fortificandum predictum ignem R(ecipe) lignum partes volgariter chyn et intinge materie predicte et suppone patellule vel crucibulo et ignis exiliet cunctis spectandis

Recipe salis nitri unc(iam) i purgati seu partes unc(ias) purgati et distillati per filtrum addendo modicum aluminis ut scis post R(ecipe) sulphuris et carbonum salicis ana partem unc(iam) et misce ut scis. Iste est pulvis cum quo intendunt pixides et mediante quibus debent inferri olea valencia pro sagittare. Item sciendum quod os patelle debet exire retro vel tanda(m) et ibi debet poni candela sulphuris incensa et sic ignis ibit versus ventum ut scis

1470s, which may have seen the use of matchlocks alongside or to the exclusion of handgonnes, are included in this study. Due to limitations of space, however, this book concentrates mainly on the development of the handgonne in Europe. Its development and replacement by the matchlock in other regions such as the Middle East and Asia deserves separate treatment elsewhere.

With regard to nomenclature, throughout the book *handgonne* is used as a general term for a pre-matchlock, hand-held black powder weapon. A *handgonner* or *gonner* refers to the person who used this weapon. In reality, handgonne was only one of many terms used. Others include *hackbut*, *couleuvrine à main*, *pistola*, *schiopetto*, *tyufyak*, and even *bombardelle*, which was usually reserved for smaller cannon but which chroniclers occasionally applied to hand-held firearms. In the weapon's early days, terms for it were vague and often interchangeable. When a specific phrase or word has been taken from a chronicle, or is otherwise known, that expression appears in this text; otherwise, the word handgonne is favoured. This is due to its generic nature, its similarity to the modern word, and its common (although not universal) use among re-enactors. The term *black powder weapons* is used to describe all weapons using gunpowder as a propellant, whether hand-held or artillery. In some places references have been made to *hundredweight*, abbreviated as cwt. This is equivalent to 50kg (about 112lb).

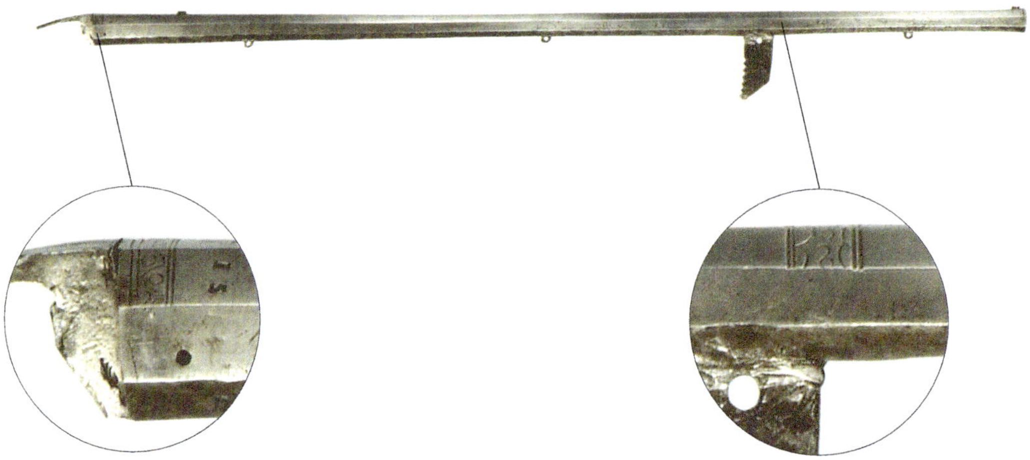

Danish handgonne, *c.*1515, or possibly earlier. This handgonne is nearly 1,500mm long. There is some simple engraved decoration on the butt end, on the top of the barrel above the hook, and on the top of the barrel above the somewhat flaring muzzle. The monogram 'IS' appears on the butt. Length 1,455mm, calibre 19.2mm, weight 10.49kg. (Danish National Museum of Military History)

DEVELOPMENT

The gunpowder revolution

The development of one of the most important substances in the history of warfare is a matter of controversy and sparse evidence. Gunpowder appears to have been invented in China in the 8th or 9th century AD and it was quickly adopted for use in bombs, grenades, rockets, and fireworks. It was a further few centuries, however, until the Chinese developed cannon and handgonnes; in other words, before they used gunpowder as a propellant rather than as an explosive. India adopted the technology next and may have had handgonnes as early as the 12th century. The Middle East seems to have started using gunpowder at about the same time.

The first recipes in Europe are found in the late 13th century. Roger Bacon gave a formula for gunpowder in the year 1267 or a little earlier in his *Epistola de Secretis Operibus Artis et Naturae, et de Nullitate Magiae* (Letter on the Secret Workings of Art and Nature, and the Vanity of Magic). Another recipe was recorded in Albert the Great's *De Mirabilibus Mundi* (Concerning the Wonders of the World), written *c.*1275. Marcus Graecus went into more detail in his *Liber Ignium ad Comburendos Hostes* (Books of Fires for the Burning of Enemies) *c.*1300. Their recipes differ in the proportion of sulphur, saltpetre, and charcoal and none of them describes a military use for the weapon, although some scholars were already thinking along those lines. In his *Opus Tertium* (Third Work), written *c.*1268, Bacon said:

> By the flash and combustion of fires, and by the horror of sounds, wonders can be wrought, and at any distance that we wish – so that a man can hardly protect himself or endure it. There is a child's toy of sound and fire made in various parts of the world with powder of saltpetre, sulphur, and charcoal of hazel wood. This powder is enclosed

> in an instrument of parchment the size of a finger, and since this can make such a noise that it seriously distresses the ears of men... If the instrument were made of solid material the violence of the explosion would be much greater.

This interesting passage not only makes a clear reference to firecrackers, probably from China, but also includes the first reference to the idea of a grenade. Graecus also mentioned fireworks and rockets.

The scholarly debate over how Europeans learned of gunpowder has lasted generations. Many believe the secret came to Europe from the Arab world via Byzantium or Spain. Others assert that Europeans independently invented the substance. To cover all aspects of this debate would take several thick volumes. Suffice to say, by the late 13th century Europeans were aware of gunpowder, its composition and properties. After 1300, references to gunpowder and recipes for it became more widespread, and it would not be long before Europeans put that knowledge to military use.

The first clear European depiction of a black powder weapon is in Walter de Milemete's *De Notabilibus Sapientiis et Prudentiis Regum* (Concerning the Majesty, Wisdom and Prudence of Kings) dating to 1326. The illustration shows a vase-shaped gun sitting on a table and firing a large arrow. The touch-hole is being lit by an armoured man using some sort of igniter on the end of a stick. It is perhaps significant that no mention of this weapon is made in the text, as if the reader is expected to know its purpose. Another book by Milemete from the same year, a copy of the pseudo-Aristotle work *De Secretis Secretorum* (About the Secret of Secrets), shows a larger example of the same device and is illustrated opposite.

This early form of cannon was called the *pot de fer* in France and *vasi* in Italy. One surviving bronze example from Loshult, Sweden, looks very similar to the Milemete gun. It is much smaller than the devices shown in the Milemete illustrations, measuring 302mm (12in) long and weighing only 9kg (20lb). Due to poor preservation its bore could not be measured exactly, but is about 30–36mm (less than 1½in). Historians date it to the 1330s or, more generally, to the early 14th century.

The projectiles for the pot de fer, called *quarrels*, *carreaux*, or *garros*, weighed anywhere from a few grams up to 90kg (200lb). They were made of iron or oak with brass or copper fletching. An account from St Omer, France, from 1342 records the making of 400 such arrows. The only surviving examples of gun arrows date from 1331 to 1333, and are kept in the German castle of Burg Eltz. Unlike a regular arrow, the fletching is halfway along the shaft, the rear half being stuck into the cannon barrel with some leather wadding. When the charge ignited, the expanding gases pushed against the rear of the shaft and sent the arrow towards the target.

In recent years, a reconstruction of the smaller of the Milemete cannons by the Royal Armouries fired an arrow weighing 1.8kg (4lb) to a range of about 150m. The arrow was 1,350mm (53in) long with a 38mm bore. A charge of only 230g (8oz) of gunpowder was found to work best, as larger charges shattered the oak shaft of the gun arrow. However, as the project was based on the sketchy evidence of a medieval

An early pot de fer or vase gun from the pseudo-Aristotle *De Secretis Secretorum*, a manuscript produced in England in 1326 by Walter de Milemete. Such a large vase gun would have been extremely heavy and some scholars have questioned if one so large was ever built. Note the gun arrow set in the muzzle ready for firing. In contrast to another Milemete image of the same year, the artist has failed to include the fletching. Note the igniter, a pole with something, perhaps a slow match, attached to the end. This is similar to the igniter in the other Milemete image. (Add.47680 f.44v, by permission of the British Library)

manuscript illustration, there were many problems in the manufacture of both the cannon and the arrow, and the experimenters themselves expressed doubt as to the validity of their reconstruction.

A replica of the Loshult gun was in 1999 also tested by the Royal Armouries and a team of Danish researchers called the Ho Group. The team used four early recipes with different proportions of saltpetre, sulphur, and charcoal. A charge of 50g (1¾oz) fired a 184g (6½oz) lead ball. A reproduction of an early gun arrow was also used with either a 20g or 50g charge. The muzzle velocity rose with the proportion of saltpetre. Gunpowder with 50 per cent saltpetre shot a lead ball with an average muzzle velocity of 110m/s, going up to 142m/s for powder containing 75 per cent saltpetre. The balls achieved ranges from 275m to 945m, the average being 630m. Two arrow shots had lower muzzle velocities, 63m/s and 87m/s, probably due to the looser fit of the projectile within the barrel, yet the arrows still achieved a range of 205m and 360m. The cannon was fired at an angle of 45 degrees, whereas in actual battle it would have almost certainly been laid level. Both contemporary images of a pot de fer show the weapon level.

The Ho Group distinguished between four different types of gunpowder. *Rough* powder is made by simply mixing the components in the proper proportions. *Meal* powder is made by mixing the dry components together, moistening the mix with alcohol (40 per cent alcohol by volume), grinding it up in a mortar and laying it out on trays to dry. It is then ground into a very fine powder. Meal powder can be made into two other variants, *fine* or *coarse incorporated* powder. Fine incorporated powder is meal powder that, when wet, is formed into small granules or corns and then allowed to dry. Coarse incorporated powder undergoes the same process but the granules or corns are larger.

Even the rough powder exploded in the tests, although it had to be tamped tightly in order to do so as previous research had found it would not explode at all if put loosely into the barrel. Meal powder was more powerful because by grinding the ingredients after dampening, rather than simply stirring, the components mixed more thoroughly. This gave more consistent muzzle velocities and a more reliable powder, as supported by contemporary literature.

Close-up of a touch-hole on the side of a 15th-century hook gun. Note the crude pan. (Foundation for Art, Culture and History, Castle of Grandson)

Test firings were also conducted with modern commercial powder. Commercial meal powder had an average muzzle velocity of 151m/s, commercial rifle powder 254m/s, and commercial cannon powder 227m/s. It is interesting to note that the 75 per cent saltpetre gunpowder made by simple hand mixing came very close in power (142m/s) to modern commercial meal gunpowder (151m/s). Medieval soldiers had effective gunpowder right from the start. However, it must be stressed that all this data came from only 19 shots, and while they show certain trends, the results must be treated with caution.

The Ho Group is unique among current researchers in that it uses powder made of materials from the original sources. For charcoal the Ho Group used alder, although willow branches are mentioned in numerous sources as the preferred wood. Marcus Graecus suggested using either willow or linden. This was the only part of the mixture that was cheap and easy to acquire.

Sulphur came from two sources in medieval Europe – Sicily and Iceland. These were the only two places in Europe where sizeable recent volcanic activity had left large amounts of sulphur readily available on the surface, and both are mentioned in contemporary documents. Not much is known about the Sicilian sulphur trade, but given its central location in the Mediterranean its influence would have been vital.

Iceland's role is better documented, and being situated on the periphery of Europe it had strong trade links with Scandinavia and England throughout the Middle Ages and the Renaissance. It was a major exporter of sulphur from at least as early as the 14th century.

The Ho Group teamed up with Icelandic archaeologists to investigate a medieval sulphur extraction site at Gásir in the northern part of the country. The sulphur in this area is so abundant that the researchers collected 50kg (110lb) from the surface with little effort. They purified it by placing it in a pan with a small amount of cooking oil and heated it gradually until it boiled. The impurities rose to the top of the bubbling mass and could be skimmed off. About half the original weight was lost in this way.

Saltpetre proved more difficult to acquire. It can occur naturally in only very precise conditions, where richly organic material is decomposing in a contained environment that encourages the development of bacteria. This generally means inside farm dung heaps and privies, or in a few

The muzzle of a 15th-century hackbut at Muider Castle, the Netherlands. Note the reinforced muzzle and chiselled decoration. Strengthening the muzzle was important because it is at this point that the expanding gases of the exploding gunpowder are at their strongest. Not all handgonnes had strengthened muzzles, however, it perhaps not being considered essential if the charge was small and the handgonne well made. This example has a larger calibre than most Dutch hackbuts, so the designer may have felt obliged to strengthen the muzzle. Length 1,815mm, calibre 33mm, weight 11.6kg. (Sean McLachlan)

naturally occurring locations. In the early days of black powder weapons, saltpetre was imported from Bengal where it was more commonly found and its characteristics better understood. The long distances involved, however, meant it was very expensive and the supply small and uncertain. Thus medieval experimenters were anxious to understand the properties of saltpetre and find more local sources, or create the conditions to encourage its natural growth.

What is generally called saltpetre can be one of two different substances – calcium nitrate or potassium nitrate. Calcium nitrate is by far the easier substance to find. It forms naturally in decomposing organic material such as manure heaps and can be extracted through the simple but rather unpleasant task of washing and precipitation. However, calcium nitrate makes poor gunpowder. The chemical compound absorbs water easily and in moist conditions gunpowder is quickly rendered useless. Some modern investigators who tried to use it in gunpowder found it wouldn't ignite at all. A way to combat the problem is to convert the substance to potassium nitrate. Besides importing potassium nitrate from Bengal, the only solution available to medieval experimenters was to figure out how to make the chemical conversion.

A 16th-century source notes a technique for converting naturally occurring calcium nitrate into potassium salt by the addition of a potassium source, such as wood ash, during the manufacturing process. This is the first direct reference to the creation of potassium nitrate, but indirect evidence shows it was actually being made a century earlier. Indeed many 15th-century references to gunpowder being spoiled by moisture indicate not that calcium nitrate was being used, but rather that the technique for converting it into potassium nitrate was imperfect, and that some calcium nitrate remained in the mixture to ruin it when it came into contact with moisture.

The Ho Group experimented with creating saltpetre and found it to be a difficult task, even when the chemical processes involved were far better known than they could have been in the Middle Ages. The researchers attempted to make saltpetre by the method of precipitation in a pit below a chicken coop, filled with alternating layers of chicken dung and lime, and covered with straw. They aerated the mass and added pig's urine to it regularly. It was then filtered through a barrel filled with layers of twigs, straw, and wood ash, before being boiled and any impurities rising to the top being skimmed away. They then boiled down the leachate until crystals formed. Analysis showed the crystals to be potassium sulphate. The Ho Group had managed to substitute potassium for calcium but not convert waste into nitrate. The group theorized that the dung heap hadn't been sufficiently aerated to encourage the growth of bacteria to break down the ammonium ions in the dung into nitrates. Also, contemporary sources stress that urine needs to be added to produce higher yields, and the group may not have put enough in. In addition, it is thought the high acidity of chicken droppings may have hampered the development of bacteria and that animal waste may have been better; indeed, 15th- and 16th-century sources mention animal or even human waste.

The pot de fer and other early cannons were small affairs, partly due to the unfamiliarity of their makers with the new technology and also the high cost of gunpowder. In England in 1347, for example, saltpetre cost 1s 6d per pound weight, and sulphur 8d. In 1379, saltpetre cost 1s 3d a pound and sulphur 6d, not a great reduction despite the increased demand. By way of comparison, an archer made 3–6d a day and a common labourer only £2 a year. Another source, dated to 1374 and detailing the construction of a cannon for the siege of Saint-Sauveur-le-Vicomte, gives the cost per pound of various materials: iron 5–6d, 'gun metal' 1s 8d, steel 10d, lead 10d, gunpowder 10s. A typical siege in the late 14th century could go through hundreds or even thousands of pounds of gunpowder.

Records from England, the Patent Rolls for Edward IV, Edward V, and Richard III, and papers for Henry VIII and Elizabeth I (tabulated below) show steadily declining prices of saltpetre over time, although it never becomes inexpensive.

Saltpetre prices in England, 1346–1599

Year	Quantity (lb)	Price per lb
1346	1,600	1s 6d (7.5p)
1396	3,900	1s 6d (7.5p)
1404	172	1s (5p)
1449	1,800	8d (3.3p)
1461	1,000	5d (2.1p)
1515	96,000	6d (2.5p)
1550	7,200	6d (2.5p)
1599	240,000	7d (2.9p)

Another problem was that imported saltpetre was often cut with cooking salt, which reduced its efficacy and necessitated a time-consuming removal process. Saltpetre would remain expensive until Europeans developed methods for making it themselves.

The Siege of Mortagne, from the *Chronique d'Angleterre*, produced in Bruges, late 15th century. The two handgonners on the left use simple weapons made of iron tubes reinforced with bands. One fires with his weapon resting on his shoulder while the other appears to tuck it under his arm. (Royal 14 E IV f.23, by permission of the British Library)

BLACK POWDER WEAPONS

Exactly when black powder weapons were first used in Europe is a matter of debate. There are possible references to cannon and even handgonnes from before 1326, but these are vague and hotly discussed by scholars. It is safe to assume, however, that if guns existed before the established date they were rare and not highly developed.

The next generation of cannon after the pot de fer were still simple affairs, built of iron bars soldered lengthwise into a tube, with the joins filled with lead or welded together. Hot iron rings would be put around the tube for reinforcement, which tightened into place as they cooled. A strong, solid piece of iron would be placed as a backing. This process so resembled barrel-making that people started using the word 'barrel' to describe the tube of the cannon. Casting cannon out of iron or bronze would have made a stronger weapon, but the process of iron casting was not sufficiently developed at that point. Bronze cannon were more expensive, but they did appear in the annals and became more common over time. Although the forged 'iron barrel' process led to weaker guns that could leak or burst, the method was relatively cheap and any repairs could be made in the field. Artillery trains included blacksmiths supplied with extra bars and rings for this purpose. Forged iron cannons continued to be popular into the 16th century, with cast bronze also being used for smaller pieces. Artillery pieces at this point were called by various names, two of the most common being *bombard* and *cannon*. At this early stage, terminology was vague and 'cannon' had not yet become a generic term.

OPPOSITE
An illustration from the Swiss *Amtliche Berner Chronik* of 1483, by Diebold Schilling. An army is besieging a fortified town, and the handgonners appear to be using button-lock arquebuses. Note the powder horn worn by the man on the right. In the centre is a cannon with adjustable mount and a box with pre-prepared charges. Crossbowmen are working in conjunction with those armed with black powder weapons, and one is winding up his crossbow with a cranequin. (Burgerbibliothek Bern, Mss.h.h.I.1, p.143)

The earliest references to black powder weapons in medieval chronicles are unfortunately sparse. In 1326 the Council of Florence is said to have ordered the manufacture of metal cannon and iron balls, but the document on which this is based may be a forgery since the person who claimed to discover it was sent to prison for stealing old documents and altering them to raise their black market value. The first passing reference to cannon being used in a siege dates back to the siege of Friuli (in Italy) in 1331. Thereafter, the English monarch Edward III brought along cannon on the Crécy campaign of 1346, as did the French who opposed him. However, the chronicles give little detail as to their construction, and contradict each other on whether cannon were actually used at the battle of Crécy on 26 August 1346. Two eyewitness accounts of the battle fail to mention them, but the chronicler Giovanni Villani, who is likely to have interviewed Genoese mercenaries who fought on the French side, relates that as the Genoese crossbowmen advanced on the English longbowmen, they were broken by repeated volleys of arrows and retreated. At this point the English set off three cannon, which so frightened the Genoese that their retreat turned into a rout.

The use of black powder weapons was more clearly recorded during the rebellion of some Flemish industrial cities, led by Philip van Artevelde of Ghent against Louis II of Flanders. At the battle of Beverhoutsveld on 3 May 1382, Louis II's force outnumbered the rebels by at least five to one, so the army from Ghent took up a defensive position with a pond on one flank and artillery on the other. Their artillery consisted of *ribaudiaux* – wheelbarrows mounted with three or more small cannons, protected from attack by long iron spikes on the front. Ribaudiaux provided both mobility and concentration of fire. Seeing the Ghentenaars' strong position, Louis II wanted to wait them out, but his allies (militiamen from Bruges) got drunk and charged the rebels in contradiction to orders. The militia had several handgonnes of an indeterminate type, but in their intoxicated state they failed to use them or any other weapon effectively. As they stumbled forward, they were met with a volley of 300 barrels from the ribaudiaux, followed by a flanking manoeuvre by the Ghentenaars around the pond. A second volley from the ribaudiaux sent the Bruges militia fleeing in panic and their fear spread to the rest of Louis II's army. The Ghentenaars moved in and slaughtered their foes, winning what might have been the first battle in which a concentration of fire from black powder weapons played a significant part.

In response to this defeat, King Charles VI of France led 10,000 men against the rebels in support of Louis II. At Comines on the river Lys, the rebels stopped them by destroying the bridge into town. The French sent knights around a bend in the river, where they could be ferried across unobserved, while the main force distracted the rebels by engaging them in an artillery duel across the water. About 400 French knights made it to the opposite bank and had to spend an uncomfortable evening in a marsh. The next day the Flemish discovered them and attacked. With both sides hampered by the mire, the fight descended into individual combat where the French knights' superior armour and training won the day. The French forced the Flemish back into Comines, at which point the main French force fixed the bridge, crossed over, and took the town.

Das die küngin von ungern einen friden und
bestant zwüschent beiden stetten macht

In den ziten als der krieg so mechtig was / under- 1340
want sich die aller durluchtigest fürstin Agnes
küngin zu ungern / und warb an beid stett
Bern und friburg das man ir gunde in die sachen
zu reden / das man ouch tet / daran kert si iren fliß
und macht ein friden und bestant von sant laurencien tag bis
sant michels tag / das ouch von beiden teilen erberlich gehalten
wart bis er wider us gieng

Das die von Bern mit gantzer
macht gon Thun zugent

OPPOSITE
Arquebusiers and crossbowmen attack a fortified town from behind a protective wall. Note the box with pre-prepared charges in the centre foreground. It is very similar to the one illustrated on page 15 for cannon, except the balls and packets of gunpowder are much smaller. Most of the arquebusiers wear full armour. From the Swiss *Amtliche Berner Chronik* of 1483, by Diebold Schilling. On the right is a partially armoured figure loading his arquebus with a ramrod. (Burgerbibliothek Bern, Mss.h.h.I.1, p.243)

The final round occurred at Roosebeke on 27 November 1382, when the rebels attacked the French with a closely ranked mass of pikemen supported by artillery and crossbowmen. The initial artillery barrage caused the French centre to waver and withdraw slightly, but as the pikes advanced the Flemish artillerists could not fire without endangering their own men. Once the pike men pushed into the indented French centre, the French flanks hit them. Pressed on three sides, the Flemish were slaughtered and their leader Philip van Artevelde died in the fray. The artillery had insufficient mobility to support the infantry effectively.

The next major battle involving the use of black powder weapons was at Aljubarrota on 14 August 1385, fought between the Portuguese and the army of the Spanish kingdom of Castile. The Portuguese had inferior numbers and took defensive positions behind a trench and brushwork palisades in order to keep the Castilian cavalry from making a charge. As an added measure they dug a chequered pattern of holes in the field in front in order to trip up their opponents' horses. Creeks and steep terrain protected their flanks. The Castilians, seeing a direct assault would be risky, deployed 16 cannon and opened up on the Portuguese position. The defenders wavered, frightened by the sight and sound of the artillery more than the effect it had on their ranks, but they did not retreat because the Castilians had already sent some light cavalry around to their rear. Having nowhere to run, the Portuguese held their ground. The Castilians finally lost patience and charged, but a determined Portuguese defence won the day. Once again black powder had struck fear in the hearts of the enemy, but failed to be the deciding factor in battle. A fixed position of relatively exposed, massed men had been able to withstand an artillery barrage.

Artillery was beginning to lose its novelty. In his *De Remediis Utriusque Fortunae* (Remedies for Fortune Fair and Foul, commonly known in English as 'Phisicke Against Fortune'), Petrach (1304–74) observed: 'This plague was only lately so rare as to be looked on as a great miracle; now, so easily taught the very worst matters are to human minds, it has become as common as any other kind of weapon.' Setting aside any medieval exaggeration (for cannon were certainly not as common as swords), the passage does suggest black powder weapons had lost their fearsomeness and now had to rely on actual deadliness.

One reason for the Castilian failure at Aljubarrota may have been insufficient firepower. If considerable numbers of Portuguese had been hit by cannon fire, they would in all probability have tried to cut their way through the Castilian cavalry as a means of escape. In Italy, the Veronese found one solution to the firepower problem during their campaign against the Paduans in 1387. They constructed a huge cart containing 144 *bombardelle* (small, portable bombards), organized into three banks of 48 guns, each bank subdivided into sets of 12 guns, all of which could be fired simultaneously or in succession, shooting stones 'the size of a hen's egg'. This contraption had a crew of three men, presumably one for each bank of guns. Like the ribaudiaux, it was an attempt to combine mobility and concentration of fire, but the cart proved too heavy to keep up with the army and failed to make it to the crucial battle of Castagnaro on 11 March 1387.

Das wesen ingenomen und gewunnen wart
Nach dem Strit von Sempach im ougste zugent 1355
die von zurich lutern vre switz vnderwalde
zug vnd Glarus für wesen vnd sturmdent daran
vnd gewunnent das mit macht vnd arbeit Und
swurent die von wesen zu den eidgnossen ein ewige punt
nisse die von Glarus hatten ouch ingenomen oder vorhin
das si darnach verbrantent

OPPOSITE
An army firing over a river. Note the wagons equipped with cannon like those in a Hussite wagenburg (see pages 46–47). The cannons in the foreground are wonderfully detailed, showing the box with pre-prepared charges, ramrod, and powder scoop. From the Swiss *Amtliche Berner Chronik* of 1483, by Diebold Schilling. (Burgerbibliothek Bern, Mss.h.h.I.1, p.347)

The reference to stones being fired is significant. Shooting giant arrows became less popular with time as soldiers discovered a smooth ball provided better accuracy. Stone was cheap and easy to shape. Lead was also favoured because it was easy to cast, but iron was less popular on account of the poor quality of cast iron at that time. In general, gonners favoured lead for smaller black powder weapons and stone for larger ones. It would have been a difficult and expensive task to cast a lead ball for the largest siege bombards.

The strengths and weaknesses of this new artillery were revealed within the first half-century of its use. It had been employed to some effect, but its major impact on the enemy, that of fear, had begun to wear off due to increased familiarity (one can imagine noblemen ordering their armies to attend artillery practice so that the loud booms and clouds of sulphurous smoke would no longer startle them). With this advantage gone, armies needed to develop new weapons that would actually be dangerous to the enemy. Large bombards, while effective in sieges, proved too slow and cumbersome for field use. Smaller cannon could be carried on wagons, but they too tended to lag behind the common soldier and could not go everywhere that he could.

The solution was to dismount the guns from the ribaudiaux and put them into the hands of individual soldiers. This offered a concentration of fire that could keep up with the marches and battlefield manoeuvres of the infantry. There had already been experiments with hand-held black powder weapons, and an inauspicious early practice session at Beverhoutsveld in 1382. The next 50 years would see this innovation put to better use.

At this point it might be interesting to consider why handgonnes were needed at all. Artillery had an obvious use in sieges, with bombards firing hundredweight balls that knocked down their first walls as early as 1375, at the siege of Saint-Sauveur-le-Vicomte. Crossbows and longbows, used for anti-personnel purposes, seemed to provide sufficient rate of fire and penetrative power compared to the slow and inaccurate early handgonnes.

Nevertheless, handgonnes must have had some advantage on the medieval battlefield, as eventually they did supplant the bow. It was a slow transition, with some armies taking a good two centuries to relinquish the longbow, preferring it even after the development of the matchlock. Yet throughout this period handgonnes were used alongside bows and crossbows, and gradually became more common than the earlier forms of missile weapons.

As the limitation of artillery in the field became obvious, it became a weapon used more exclusively for sieges. Cannon grew in size, their builders gaining confidence, and soon they were regularly engaged in battering down city and castle walls. Smaller cannon were still being used for the defence of fortified positions and in the field of battle, but now the smallest black powder weapons, handgonnes, came to the fore. They used little powder, cost less, and proved more useful in the field.

Just as this transition was occurring in the late 14th century, gunpowder began to get cheaper as Europeans learned to manufacture

Das die Burgunner lamparter vnd Pickar
ten mit grossen maisten / an die von
Bernn vnd annder / In witem volcke
kament vnd si nit getorsten angriffen

OPPOSITE
A fortified town under siege. The attackers are using a rather primitive bombard, considering the period, as well as arrows with something attached to their ends – probably incendiary devices. The defenders have their handgonnes hooked against the wall to steady their aim. From the Swiss *Amtliche Berner Chronik* of 1483, by Diebold Schilling. (Burgerbibliothek Bern, Mss.h.h.I.1, p.739)

their own saltpetre. The first recorded saltpetre plantation opened in Frankfurt in 1388 and others soon appeared elsewhere in Europe. These plantations usually comprised cellars or pits filled with straw, leaves, and slaked lime, which were kept at a constant temperature for about a year in order to promote the natural formation of calcium nitrate. The plantations were watered regularly with urine from animals or a 'wine-drinking man'. This curious last element relates to the increased level of ammonia in the urine of a person who has been drinking heavily. It is significant because in the final stage of decomposition, bacteria metabolizes ammonia into nitrites and nitrates. While bacteria can get ammonia from the waste products of other micro-organisms, adding an extra supply speeds up the process, something gunpowder researcher Bert Hall referred to as 'fertilizing the fertilizer pile'.

Recipes for gunpowder dating to the 14th and 15th centuries give varying proportions of saltpetre, sulphur, and charcoal – allowing for the differences in the purity of saltpetre and the type of black powder weapon for which the gunpowder was intended. Even with the new saltpetre plantations purity could not be assured, for techniques were relatively primitive and producers had only a vague notion of the chemical processes involved. Gonners generally mixed powder themselves as poorly prepared powder could be understrength or, more seriously, overstrength. While the danger of using early black powder weapons has been overstated in much of the literature, the number of references to, and examples of, split barrels suggests that being a gonner was not a job for the faint-hearted.

Domestic saltpetre manufacture led to cheaper gunpowder and allowed for larger cannon and more numerous handgonnes. Contemporary records show a huge increase in gunpowder stores through the 15th century. Whereas 14th-century records describe small quantities, usually in the dozens of pounds, and contain numerous urgent requests for more, in the 15th century the amounts steadily rise. In France, the castle of Melun needed only 10.5kg (23lb) of gunpowder in 1359, but by 1371 the castle of Breteuil needed 45kg (100lb). A major siege like that of Saint-Sauveur-le-Vicomte in 1375 required 90kg (200lb). At that time there were few handgonnes, and only a small number of cannon that were slow-firing and generally small. But in 1448, less than a century later, the Duke of Burgundy sent the Knights Hospitaller 1,633kg (3,600lb) of powder to defend Rhodes against the Sultan of Egypt. In 1430 the Burgundians needed 7,711kg (17,000lb) to fight Joan of Arc's army.

These large supplies were necessary. While a fortified town or castle could not withstand an artillery bombardment for ever, it still took quite a few hits to bring the walls tumbling down. During the week-long siege of Dinant (in Belgium) in 1466, the attackers fired more than 1,700 cannon balls. The besiegers of Lagny (in France) in 1431 fired 412 stone cannon balls in a single day. Commanders besieging fortifications would try to parley with the defenders in order to save time and money. They would have worried about running out of gunpowder before the walls could be breached. This was demonstrated in 1475, when the Burgundians failed to take Cologne because their stocks were exhausted.

Das etlich zedel von den Burgunnern
In murten an pfilen geschossen wurde

At 14th-century prices, this vast expenditure of powder would have been beyond the means of even the wealthiest kingdoms, but cheaper powder had encouraged the greater use of guns, which in turn increased the demand for powder. A major industry sprang up to fulfil this demand. Estimates of early 15th-century artillery charges state that a large bombard needed 36kg (80lb) of powder per shot, while a *veuglaire* (a mid-sized cannon) needed 18kg (40lb), and a *couleuvrine* needed 10kg (22lb). Thus a single shot from the smallest cannon in the early 15th century would have used almost the entire supply held at the castle of Melun less than 100 years before. The gunpowder requirements of an army's handgonners were minuscule compared with those of the artillery train.

Cheaper gunpowder also democratized the handgonne. In the early 15th century, the handgonne was the weapon of choice for the peasant Hussites when they rebelled against the Holy Roman Empire. Even before this, commoners had used small cannon or handgonnes in an attack on Huntercombe Manor in England in 1375. Gunpowder was now plentiful, its recipe no longer a secret to be written in code, and it was within the means of most people. The handgonne was a simple weapon that could be made by any village blacksmith, who needed only to heat a flat portion of iron and roll it into a tube, then drill a pan and touch-hole into it. Finishing with a hammer and file made the handgonne ready for use. Casting such a simple shape was not beyond a village blacksmith's abilities either.

Despite the lowered cost, military leaders still considered gunpowder, handgonnes, and artillery as important prizes of war. In 1423, during the Hundred Years' War, the agreement surrendering the French town of Le Crotoy to Anglo-Burgundian forces stipulated that the defenders give up all their gunpowder and firearms. No other type of weapon was included in this agreement. Numerous other documents show that commanders considered the capture of an enemy artillery train to be a major coup. There was a constant need for more gunpowder, artillery, and to a lesser extent handgonnes, and an army that fell behind with supplies could end up defeated.

Increased familiarity and experience with gunpowder meant that by about 1400, gunpowder recipes tended to be close to the ideal proportions of ingredients – 75 per cent saltpetre, 12 per cent sulphur, and 13 per cent charcoal. One of the most popular recipes at this time called for proportions of 71 per cent/13 per cent/16 per cent.

Handgonnes had become useful tools in battle, but remained limited in power and versatility until new innovations in gunpowder in the early 15th century – crumbled and corned powder – brought them to the next level. The first reference to the new technique dates to *c.*1407, although it may have been developed in England as early as 1372. Up until this time gunpowder had been made into a finely milled substance sometimes referred to as *serpentine* or, as already described, mealed powder. Flame in gunpowder spreads when the surface of burning grains lets out a fine shower of sparks that hits other grains and sets them alight. With such fine powder, the surface area of the grains is too small to allow the flame to spread efficiently. Artillerists and handgonners did not understand the principle behind this, but did discover that if they packed the powder too tightly, it would not ignite at all due to lack of oxygen. Packing the powder too loosely resulted in an inefficient ignition. Thus they packed powder chambers only partially full, allowing the grains to be somewhat loose, with oxygen in between. Trial and error, rather than any sound knowledge of the chemical and physical processes involved, led to this development.

Another problem with early mealed powder was that the components easily separated out during transport. Gonners had to carry sulphur, saltpetre, and charcoal separately, and mix them in the field – not the most desirable situation given the chance for surprise encounters and inclement weather.

A third problem was that saltpetre decayed quickly in moist conditions. Early saltpetre included a proportion of calcium nitrate, also known as *lime saltpetre*, because the properties of the saltpetre plantations leached out the natural calcium of the decaying matter and surrounding soil. Workers often added plaster or ground seashell as they found it produced richer yields. Thus the majority of the nitrates produced would be calcium nitrates. But calcium nitrate is very hygroscopic (a good absorber of ambient moisture). Given the humid conditions of much of Europe, this proved to be a major problem, and saltpetre quickly dissolved unless handled with great care.

Medieval munitions experts found that if gunpowder was moistened and made into a cake and left to dry, the resultant hard cake would have a low surface-to-volume ratio. Not only would the cake be more resistant to moisture than fine-grained powder, but it could be transported without separating into its component parts. The cake would have to be crumbled to be usable, and the resultant grains were larger than mealed powder. These *crumbed* or *crumbled* grains had a lower surface-to-volume ratio, and thus absorbed less damp from the air. In addition, during the mixing process the saltpetre would dissolve in the water and enter the porous charcoal, where it was less likely to separate even after being crumbled.

Different recipes call for different liquids to be used. Some require water, others pig's urine, vinegar, brandy, wine, or the urine of a 'wine-drinking man'. In fact only water is necessary, but any liquid will do as there is no further chemical process from any of the above liquids that would improve the powder. While the increased ammonia level in a heavy drinker helps create saltpetre in a dung heap, it does nothing to existing saltpetre. Professor Hall suggested the gunpowder makers worked from a misplaced analogy, that since a drunkard's urine helps makes saltpetre, it would help them make better gunpowder.

Not only did this crumbled powder last longer in storage, it burned more quickly and thus increased the ballistic power of the weapon. Gonners quickly adopted crumbled powder and its use became almost universal by 1420. The results of this discovery had profound applications.

The first description of crumbled powder appears in the famous *Feuerwerkbuch* (Firework Book), a treatise for artillerists written in the second decade of the 15th century, which used material dating back to a couple of decades earlier. The anonymous author boasted that two pounds

A very early depiction of a matchlock. This simple serpentine is from Johann Hartlieb's *Kriegsbuch*, dated 1411. While it would seem this major innovation would spread quickly, handgonnes without matchlocks can be seen in artwork dating to 60 years after this image. The man on the right appears to be pouring molten lead into bullet moulds. (Austrian National Library, Vienna, Picture Archive, Cod. MS 3069, f.38v)

of crumbled powder equalled the strength of three pounds of mealed powder. The French version of the book says the ratio is 1:3, perhaps reflecting a better process in what was one of Europe's most advanced regions for black powder weapon development. This extra strength presented a problem for artillery, as a cannon had a relatively thin barrel in comparison to the size of the charge. Continuing to use mealed powder, mixing crumbled and mealed powders, and reducing the proportion of saltpetre when making crumbled powder were three methods used to reduce the powder's strength. However, cutting the saltpetre content of crumbled powder still gave a powder that was stronger and more easily transportable than mealed powder, and also lowered the cost, since saltpetre was still the most expensive ingredient even with domestic manufacture. Smaller cannon grew more popular, especially those with longer barrels that allowed the powder to gain maximum force as it pushed the ball along.

Countermeasures

Black powder weapons had a profound influence on castle construction. By the late 14th century every siege involved an artillery bombardment. Handgonnes were less effective in sieges since they could not punch through walls like the larger cannons could, but illuminated manuscripts frequently show them being used as anti-personnel weapons by attackers and defenders alike. Handgonners would often fire from atop the battlements, but they also used arrow slits that had been altered to accommodate their needs. A round opening at the bottom of the slit would be cut out to make an 'inverted keyhole' shape.

On later castles inverted keyholes were specifically built for gonnes, the vertical slit acting as a viewing space. While this was the most common form, many others existed. Some were 'dumb-bell' shaped, for gonnes mounted in pairs or to give a single gonne a wider field of fire. There were also circular openings made in the middle of a slit instead of at the bottom. Another form was the 'letterbox' port that was circular on the inside and appeared as a horizontal slit on the outside. The first recorded addition of gun ports to an English fortification was in 1365–66 at Quarr Abbey on the Isle of Wight, by which time they were already in use in continental Europe. Gun ports appeared in greater frequency until they became standard in castles by the mid-15th century. Some strongholds had only a few, while others had a great number. Raglan Castle in Wales, started in the year 1435, had 32, a large number for the time.

The majority of gun ports were cut no higher than a metre from the inside floor, indicating that the gonner had to sit or kneel to fire. Most gun ports allowed less than a 45-degree angle of fire. Their small size (the circular openings rarely being more than 300mm in diameter and often half that) suggests that only handgonnes or small cannons such as couleuvrines could have been fired from them.

Other gun ports were clearly designed for handgonnes. The interior would have square sockets on either side of the gun port opening to hold a wooden crossbeam on which to hook a hackbut (also known as a *hook* gun). These are found at Winchester Castle, and the Dutch castles of Doornenburg and Muider, among others.

It is often said that the invention of the handgonne eliminated the usefulness of armour and led to its abandonment. While this may have been true in the long run, handgonnes did not immediately affect the armour-wearing habits of the medieval soldier. For although handgonnes had good penetrative power at short range, this power reduced rapidly at longer ranges, as did accuracy. Also, the vast majority of weapons a soldier would encounter – swords, polearms, even arrows – could still be deflected by good plate armour. It was only in the 16th century, when handgonners carried more accurate matchlocks with more powerful gunpowder, and had organized themselves into large units, that armour began to be reduced and was eventually dispensed with entirely.

ABOVE Arrow slit with gun port, Muider Castle, the Netherlands. This castle dates to 1370 but was modified numerous times, so it is unclear when gun ports were added to all the arrow slits. (Sean McLachlan)

ABOVE A 15th-century hackbut positioned for firing at a gun port at Muider Castle, the Netherlands. Note the wooden crossbeam, now somewhat decayed, on which the hackbut could be braced. (Sean McLachlan)

This Flemish or French tapestry shows a gonner firing a couleuvrine. The term could refer to a handgonne (usually called a couleuvrine à main) or a small cannon. This elaborate piece has a wheeled carriage and a system for fixing elevation. The gonner is shielding his face from potential powder burns. (Courtesy David Nicolle)

Crumbled powder remained a short-term problem for artillery until the latter part of the 15th century, when a new technique became popular. Gunpowder makers began to push the cakes through a sieve to get regularly shaped grains that were smaller and smoother than the irregular grains of crumbled powder but were larger than the tiny particles of mealed powder. This *corned* powder burned quickly and evenly, but did not burn as fast as crumbled powder and thus was not as strong. It resisted damp better than mealed powder, was suitable for cannon, and could be carried premixed without fear of separation.

Crumbled powder revolutionized the handgonne. Hand-held weapons had thicker barrels in relation to their calibre and powder charge, and were thus proportionally stronger than artillery. In the mealed powder era, handgonne barrels had to remain short to compensate for the weaker expansive properties of primitive powder, but now they could be made longer to maximize the gas expansion of a more powerful powder.

With the new powder, the expanding gas had more time to accelerate the ball. As the ball's kinetic energy is a function of the square of the velocity, even a modest increase in barrel length had a noticeable effect on a ball's penetrative power. Longer barrel length also provided greater accuracy and range. Crumbled or crumbed powder became the powder of choice for handgonners, and documents often list it stored alongside handgonnes.

By the 1470s, or perhaps earlier, handgonne barrels became forged iron pieces, about a metre long, with a short wooden stock that could be braced against the elbow or shoulder as the handgonner lit the weapon with a slow match. The addition of a matchlock, sometimes confusingly called a serpentine due to its shape rather than the type of gunpowder used, created what now truly looked like a modern firearm. The longer barrel contained the gas as the ball moved towards the muzzle, building up pressure to such an extent that the ball emerged at supersonic velocity. Modern tests show a muzzle velocity of 450m/s. The greater penetrative power of these weapons can be imagined. Bullets became smaller, generally 12–15mm rather than the 20–25mm of the hackbut, but much deadlier.

This velocity was not possible with the earlier mealed powder, even in a short barrel, let alone with a longer one. The Italian metallurgist Vannoccio Biringuccio, writing in the early 16th century, said that if artillery powder were used in an arquebus, it would scarcely push the ball 'fifteen feet' (4.5m) out of the barrel. This would be the case if he were talking about mealed (serpentine) or perhaps even corned powder.

Thus soldiers soon had matchlock arquebuses, forged in a cheap and simple process and fired with portable and affordable powder. The two great advantages of the handgonne, simplicity and low cost, were inherited by its deadlier descendant. At this point the handgonne was in many ways perfected. While better locks would be developed, and rifling would increase range and accuracy, the basic design would remain the same to this day.

An interesting study could be made of the relationship between the crossbow and the handgonne. They are frequently found being used side by side in the chronicles, with the proportion gradually changing in favour of the handgonne. Some writers have speculated that the rapid increase in the strength of the crossbow during the 15th century was due to competition from the handgonne, which modern tests have shown to have had better penetrative power. The crossbow's draw became stronger, and a weapon that could once be drawn by putting a foot in a stirrup at the end while pulling on the string by hand developed a range of devices to pull heavier and heavier draws, until at last there came the steel crossbow requiring a windlass with hooked cords and double crank-handles called a *cranequin*. While this arms race increased the crossbow's ability to penetrate armour, it also slowed down its handling at the very time that handgonners in some areas were being supplied with matchlocks and premeasured cartridges that sped up their reloading. Both weapons required little training, but the handgonne remained the cheaper option and eventually prevailed.

USE

Firearms on the medieval battlefield

TYPES OF HANDGONNE

Handgonnes appeared as three distinct types, detailed below, ranging from simple to relatively complex. While it would be tempting to see these as three discrete developmental phases, the dating of these types is extremely difficult. The vast majority of handgonnes preserved in public or private collections have no information as to their specific origins, some having been excavated as stray finds. Several have been found in moats, where they would have been tossed after the barrel burst. Illustrations in illuminated manuscripts and other medieval art, while relatively easy to date, show a mixture of handgonnes being used at the same time. So while a rough chronology is given here for the sake of clarity, it must by no means be considered absolute.

The first and apparently earliest type of handgonne consisted of a short bronze or iron barrel mounted on a much longer wooden pole. The section of the exterior of the barrel could be round, hexagonal, or octagonal. The muzzle was sometimes thickened to form a ring, reinforcing the point at which the escaping gases would be at their strongest. The touch-hole was set near the rear end of the barrel at the top and was rarely fitted with any sort of pan, rather being a simple cup with a vent hole leading down to the charge. Later examples, tentatively dated to the early 15th century, had a proper firing pan, deep and usually fitted at the side of the barrel and supplied with a pivoting cover. This made firing easier and helped keep the powder dry, so it was an important development even if it does not seem to have been universally adopted.

A man firing a large handgonne of the socketed variety, from Konrad Kyeser's *Bellifortis*, *c.*1405. Note that he is holding the stock with both hands as sparks come out of the touch-hole. Perhaps this indicates that a second man, not shown, has lit it. (Niedersächsische Staats- und Universitätsbibliothek Göttingen)

Two methods are known to have been used to attach the barrel to the pole. The first used a wooden stock, the front part of which was somewhat wider than the barrel and grooved at the top. The barrel rested in this groove and was held in place by one or more iron bands, thus resembling a smaller version of an early cannon. This suggests it was the first type to be developed and explains the common term *hand cannon*. The second

An army attacking a castle with handgonnes and cannon, *c.*1468. The attackers and defenders use simple handgonnes of the socketed variety. While the stocks seem to be iron, since they are painted the same colour as the barrels, the weapons do not appear to be hackbuts for they lack hooks. The simple socketed handgonne therefore appears to have been in use a full 100 years or more after its introduction. (Burney MS 169 f.127, by permission of the British Library)

method involved a wooden pole that fitted into a socket at the rear end of the barrel. In both cases a hook was often attached near the front end to be used as a brace when firing from a wall, trestle, or even in the field using a fork or *pavise* (large shield) stuck into the ground. The hook could either be cast as part of the barrel, welded onto it, fitted onto the barrel with a clamp, fitted onto the stock with a clamp, or set into the stock. Since many handgonnes of this type lost their stocks over the centuries, it is impossible to say which method was the most common.

This first type of handgonne varied widely in dimensions, although most weapons were small. One grooved example, the 'Berner Büchse', tentatively dated to *c.*1400, has a round iron barrel 180mm (7in) long, a calibre of 30mm, and a hook for bracing the weapon while firing. An early socketed example, the 'Tannenberg gun', came from the ruins of Tannenberg Castle, Hessen. This castle was torn down after a siege in

A small early handgonne of the grooved type, dated by the museum to the 14th/15th century. Purchased from a Croatian collector but provenance unknown. The stock is modern. Barrel length 160mm, calibre 18mm, weight 1.55kg. (Croatian History Museum)

1399, so the handgonne predates this. Its hexagonal barrel is made of cast bronze and is 320mm (12in) long with a calibre of 17.5mm. It weighs 1.24kg (2¾lb), but the stock has been lost.

While handgonnes with either grooved or socketed stocks were generally small, those of the socketed subtype could sometimes be quite large. An illustration in Konrad Kyeser's *Bellifortis* ('Strong in War'), a manuscript dating to *c.*1405, shows a large example with its butt end set into the ground and the barrel resting on a forked support. This handgonne was not fitted with a hook, probably because it was too big to hold level.

Although socketed handgonnes appeared quite early, they continued to be seen in manuscript illustrations as late as the 1470s, a remarkably long lifespan carrying well into the period when later types of handgonne had become widespread. It appears the socketed form was relatively effective, and perhaps ease of manufacture encouraged gunsmiths to continue making it.

The next type of handgonne had a thin metal tiller, used to brace the weapon for firing, made as one piece along with a thicker barrel. It was usually made entirely of iron, although bronze examples were known. The tiller was generally circular or square in section and usually terminated in a ring, placed either horizontally or vertically. The barrel could be circular, hexagonal, or octagonal in section, and comprised about one-quarter or one-fifth of the total length of the handgonne. The touch-hole could be on the top or the side, a simple cup or a proper pan with or without a swivelling lid. A hook was either fitted onto the barrel by a band, or made as one with the entire piece. The hook was almost universal on this type of handgonne, and the few examples that do not have them may have lost them. This signature feature gave this type of handgonne the name *hackbut*, (also known as *Hakenbüchse*, or *haquebut*), referring to the hook. The French term, *arquebus*, eventually became the most favoured. Similar to the earlier grooved and socketed handgonnes, the muzzle is either the same size as the rest of the barrel or sometimes thickened to form a ring.

The tiller was generally straight, but some have been found that were bent. While some of these may have been damaged by the vagaries of time, there seems to have been a trend towards tillers that bent upwards at their very end. These appear in a few contemporary drawings of horsemen firing with the bent tiller resting against the chest. Confusingly, some examples with this bent tiller are well over a metre in length, and would

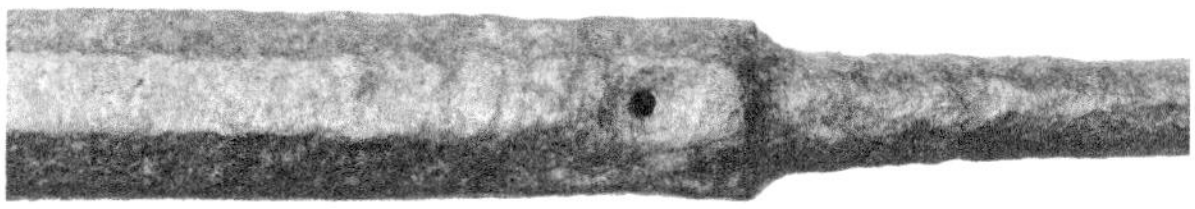

Iron hackbut from the Low Countries, *c.*1500, formerly in the collection of Mr van den Brink, Utrecht, Holland, it was reportedly dredged up from either the river Rijn or Waal. The muzzle is slightly flared. The barrel is circular in section at the front before becoming hexagonal near the back. It has a hook forged as one with it. The tiller is circular in section and sweeps upwards into a pear-shaped loop. Overall length 1,295mm, length of barrel 710mm, length of haft 585mm, length of hook 75mm, calibre 20mm, weight 5.5kg.

INSET
Close-up of the touch-hole, located on the top of the barrel. (Courtesy Royal Armouries)

not have been practical to use on horseback. Contemporary illustrations of mounted handgonners always show them firing rather short weapons.

Some larger specimens of hackbuts were equipped with a long pin attached to the barrel some distance behind the hook. Presumably this was set into a hole or bracket on a wall or ship, and would provide a stable anchor as the hackbut was turned this way and that. If the hackbut needed to be moved elsewhere, the handgonner could simply lift it out of its holder, carry it to the new location, and use the hook to brace it as he would any other hackbut. One researcher has suggested these pins were later additions. It is possible that older hackbuts were re-used as swivel guns aboard ships.

There are considerably more hackbuts surviving in collections than grooved or socketed handgonnes. This is no doubt due to their increased popularity, a fact supported by the documentary evidence. Hackbuts date back to the 15th century. Handgonnes by this phase had become almost universal in Europe and even the arsenals of relatively unimportant cities and towns included at least a few.

An analysis of 30 hackbuts in the Netherlands reveals some interesting data. They vary considerably in weight, from 5.5kg to 20kg (12–44lb), but the majority range from 10kg to 16kg (22–35lb). Calibres are 20mm, 26mm, 28mm, 30mm, and 33mm. That every one of these calibres has at least four examples indicates some attempt at standardization. With larger numbers of handgonnes coming into use, this would have made things much simpler for those making the bullets.

Length is even more standardized, with the majority between 1,000mm and 1,100mm (39–43in), although three are about 1,200mm (47in), and two others measure 600mm (23½in) and 710mm (28in). Only seven of the 30 examples have the touch-hole on the side of the barrel, and always on the right side, the rest being on the top. It has been suggested that those with the touch-hole on the side are later models, and while this makes sense developmentally there is no hard evidence to support this idea. All the barrels are octagonal along their entire length or at least part of the length, except for a single specimen that has a hexagonal barrel.

The ring at the end of the tiller is a bit of a mystery. In the case of horsemen, contemporary illustrations show the ring to have been used to attach the handgonne to a hook in the handgonner's breastplate, but some weapons are too long for this to be practical. End rings seem evenly divided between being horizontally or vertically placed. In two of the Dutch cases there is a button instead of a ring, and in both of these the tiller turns upwards at the end; in a British example it turns downwards.

There has been much speculation as to what these differences might mean, but there is the distinct possibility that the vertical and horizontal rings had the same use.

Another mystery is the common occurrence of a horizontal hole, generally about 20mm in diameter, drilled through the tiller 100–200mm behind the barrel. A manuscript dated 1460–80 from the Royal University Library in Erlangen (Germany) shows hackbuts with a pivoting lever attached to the tiller, and this may be the origin of the hole. The front end of this lever had a match holder, and was therefore a simple serpentine matchlock. Another possibility is that handgonners tied one end of their slow match around this hole, keeping the match in a secure location close to the touch-hole. Unfortunately, no pivot or slow match has been found actually attached to one of these holes.

Aiming devices were uncommon on early handgonnes. One reason for this may be that the weapons were too inaccurate to warrant their use, but it may also have been due to the danger of putting one's eye so close to the touch-hole or firing pan. Aiming devices were all but unknown in

Hackbut, 15th century, from the Low Countries, with a 614mm swivel pin for placing in an embrasure on a wall or ship. There is a button sight on the muzzle. The touch-hole is on the top of the octagonal barrel. The red paint is probably later in date, but sources mention that some of the Burgundian artillery was painted red. Paint would help prevent rusting. Length 1,960mm, calibre 28mm, weight 16.9kg. (Legermuseum, Delft)

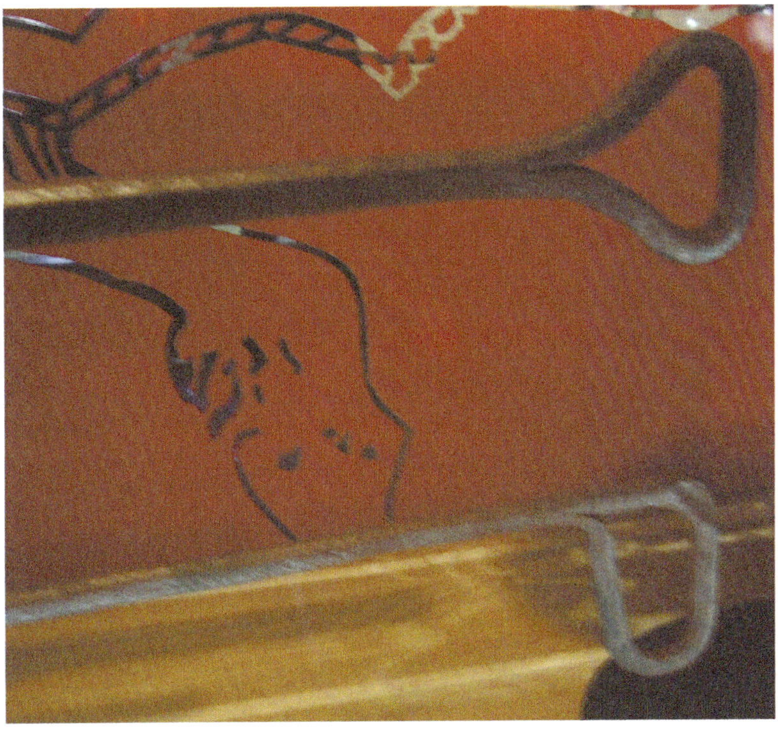

Tiller ends of two 15th-century hackbuts in Muider Castle, the Netherlands. The loops on both of these examples are vertical, but horizontal loops are equally common. The loops come in various shapes. (Sean McLachlan)

the socketed and grooved varieties but became more common with hackbuts. At least seven of the analysed Dutch hackbuts have a front or rear sight.

A smaller collection of hackbuts from the Heeresgeschichtliches Museum in Vienna shows similar measurements to those in the Netherlands collection. One is 1,010mm long, with a calibre of 23mm and a weight of 8.86kg. The next is 1,195mm long, calibre 24mm and 11.93kg. Another is 1,515mm long, calibre 21mm and 13.4kg.

The siege of Constantinople (previous pages)

The siege of Constantinople in 1453 saw the use of a variety of cannons and handgonnes on both sides. The siege is famous for the large cannon that helped the Ottoman Sultan Mehmet II 'The Conqueror' batter through the strong land walls of Constantinople. It was said to fire a ball weighing 1,212lb (550kg). In addition to this behemoth, one source said the Ottomans had 68 more artillery pieces of various sizes keeping up a steady fire. The Byzantines and their allies from the Italian city-states had several cannon of their own, mostly used as anti-personnel weapons firing clusters of five to ten bullets each the size of a walnut. Less well known are the numerous handgonnes used by both sides. Very little is said about these weapons, so this reproduction must rely upon some speculation.

We know from Turkish sources of the 14th and 15th century that the Byzantines had handgonnes. Since the Byzantine Empire was impoverished by the time of the siege of 1453, we can theorize that its soldiers would not have had many of the latest serpentine- and button-lock arquebuses that were then coming into vogue. Indeed, French chronicles from the 1460s show French troops still using the old socketed style of handgonne, so it is not hard to believe that a bankrupt state such as Byzantium would be using the older styles.

A group of 700 Genoese troops led by Giovanni Giustiniani Longo arrived to help Constantinople in its hour of need. The chronicles say that they were well armed and armoured, and since Italy was one of the regions at the forefront of black powder weapon development, the Genoese shown here are armed with serpentine arquebuses. The Genoese leader was mortally wounded by a bullet during the final Ottoman assault. This so dispirited his troops that they retreated, allowing the Ottomans to break into the city. This is surely one of the most historically important deaths by handgonne in the annals of warfare.

The Ottomans, too, were quick to adopt the arquebus in its latest form. They imported handgonnes from Italy and became adept at making them themselves. In addition to serpentines, they may have had button-lock arquebuses by this time. In this image we see Ottoman troops attacking a breach in the inner land wall of Constantinople. They are supported by arquebusiers with button-lock arquebuses. The Byzantine and Italian defenders have hastily erected a barrier across the breach. From right to left we see a variety of handgonnes in use.

First are a pair of Byzantine handgonners. One holds a shield on which the second braces and aims a pre-matchlock handgonne. The shield-bearer lights the handgonne with a slow match. Next we see a Byzantine firing a similar handgonne, this time braced under his arm. Both of the Byzantine handgonnes are of the common 'hackbut' type seen throughout Europe in the 15th century. To the left of the Byzantines are a pair of Italians with simple serpentine handgonnes. As we have seen from illustrations elsewhere in this book, this simple device for putting the match into the firing pan appeared at least 40 years before the siege of Constantinople, but earlier styles of pre-matchlock handgonne continued to be used until the end of the 15th century.

After the hackbut came the third type of handgonne. It looked more like a modern gun and was certainly developed later than the previous two, although the types overlapped in time. The shoulder stock appeared sometime in the mid-15th century, probably as a result of the first serpentine matchlocks being fitted onto the weapons. This was shorter and thicker than the slim iron tiller of the hackbut, and flared somewhat at the back so it could rest more comfortably against the hip or shoulder. The stock reverted to wood, and the barrel became longer and thinner thanks to improved powder providing better ballistics. Despite this innovation, the two earlier types of handgonne continued for some time, and the matchlock did not become universal in Europe until well into the 16th century.

Makers of handgonnes gradually learned that longer barrels allowed the gas to reach maximum expansion before the ball left the muzzle. Early mealed powder had little expansive power so barrels remained short, but with the introduction of crumbled and corned powder it behoved the gonnemaker to lengthen the barrel and take advantage of the new powder's greater expansion qualities.

All three types of handgonne were rough-and-ready pieces. Very few showed any real artistry in their decoration. One exception, the Mørkø handgonne from Sweden, a socketed weapon, is fitted with a little head behind the touch-hole that may have had a practical use in holding the match. Some other pieces have simple decorations such as etched lines or makers' marks. These were commoners' weapons, and no ornately decorated examples embossed with silver and gold have survived to show they were ever considered symbols of status like some later flintlocks.

EARLY USE

Perhaps the earliest reference to the mass use of handgonnes is the purchase of 500 of these weapons (of an indeterminate type) by the town of Perugia, Italy, in 1364. Other than the detail that they could be used by an individual soldier, there is no discussion of their appearance, but they were probably the simple socketed or grooved type. Such an investment at a time when gunpowder was still quite expensive shows that the military leaders of Perugia had confidence in the effectiveness of these weapons. At this early stage black powder weapons were still something of a novelty, and one can imagine the effect on the opposing force when faced with a volley of 500 handgonnes.

An early handgonne, *c.*1400, found by a 'mudlark' in the Thames foreshore. Note the reinforced muzzle and wires for strengthening the barrel. (Courtesy Royal Armouries)

The Vedelspang gun, an early handgonne from Denmark, found in the moat of Vedelspang Castle, Schleswig-Holstein, Germany. The castle was built in 1416 and demolished in 1426, so presumably this piece dates to within that time. The hook is clamped on and the tiller ends in a knob. The octagonal barrel has burst, making it difficult to determine the calibre, but the bore appears to be slightly conical, widening towards the muzzle. Overall length 810mm, barrel length 210mm, calibre 18–27mm, weight 2.44kg. (Danish National Museum of Military History)

Handgonnes were simple to make and use, and this helped them to spread even among poorer areas. The first recorded use of handgonnes in battle in England was in 1375 when rioters broke into Huntercombe Manor. That commoners used these weapons against their superiors was significant – they were losing their mystery and exclusivity. Nor would the rioters at Huntercombe Manor be the last commoners to use them in rebellion.

Handgonnes first appeared in the accounts of the English king's privy wardrobe in the following decade, although they may have been present in the arsenal before that and simply not distinguished in the records. There is even a reference to a 'handgone' from 1338, but the actual date of these records has been debated. Accounts rarely give much detail about handgonnes other than their cost and numbers, and sometimes not even that. A record from the Privy Wardrobe of the Tower of London from

The Handgonner's Experience

While much can be learned from contemporary accounts, what was it really like to fire a handgonne in battle? Pre-matchlock and early matchlock firearms are popular among re-enactors and their personal experiences are invaluable. Caution must be used, however, in drawing too close a parallel between a re-enactor's experience and that of an actual soldier, because the majority of re-enactors use modern gunpowder and, of course, none of them are shooting in a real battle. When firing, one has to be careful when applying a match to the priming in order not to get burned. The best method is to curve the match somewhat and hold the hand behind and a little below the pan. At worst the hand will get a slight singeing, probably not even noticeable to a rough medieval soldier with calloused hands. A thin pair of gloves protects the hands completely. One re-enactor related that in more than 100 shots, he had never suffered a serious burn.

An interesting observation by some re-enactors using replicas of early matchlocks was that the slow match has to be constantly adjusted in its holder (often called a *dog*) or it runs the risk of missing the pan. Sometimes rough handling makes the match fall off its holder. In the heat of simulated battle, it can be quicker and easier to simply stick the match in by hand, not using the matchlock function at all. Indeed, there are a few period illustrations showing soldiers doing just that, such as in the 1533 *Siege of Alesia* by Melchior Feselen, hanging in the Alte Pinakothek, Munich (and reproduced on page 73).

Sighting is a more dangerous matter. One cannot sight down the barrel with any degree of safety as the flash from the pan can cause serious eye injury. It is best to sight down the side or simply gauge it by 'feel'. This brings into question the sighting marks found on many early hackbuts. Did handgonners risk blindness for the sake of a better shot?

One common complaint by re-enactors is that some models of handgonnes do not have a proper pan, simply a shallow cup-shaped touch-hole, and this often leads to the priming powder being shaken or blown off. The rapid development of a deep firing pan, often with a swivelling cover, is no surprise considering this serious problem.

1388 gives the stark description of 'three small cannon of brass, called handgonnes'. That handgonnes were considered 'small cannon' makes one wonder how many of the other 'small cannon' that appear in early records were in fact handgonnes. An earlier entry dating to between 1373 and 1375 mentions putting handles on eight 'gunnorum'. The fact that some hatchets were fitted with identical handles at the same time hints that these 'gunnorum' were actually handgonnes.

The English were certainly eager to adopt black powder weapons. A hundred *ribalds* (by which the clerks probably meant ribaudiaux) had been made in the Tower of London as early as 1345. Each cost only a little more than £1, and this included their transport from London across the Channel. Thus a handgonne, which was essentially a single dismounted barrel of a ribaudiaux, would have been within the budget of many commoners.

There has been some scholarly debate as to when the slow match, a cord impregnated with saltpetre, first came into use. When lit, this match would glow but not give flame, and would burn slowly down the length of the cord. Many scholars claim slow matches did not appear until the early 15th century, and that earlier black powder weapons were fired using a red-hot wire. While many early depictions show artillerists and handgonners igniting their weapons with something drawn only as a thin black line, it is questionable whether a hot wire would have been practical. It would have required a brazier of coals or a campfire to keep it hot, although the latter option would have been a bad idea for obvious reasons. A brazier would have been no impediment to the crew of a fixed cannon; however, while a handgonner defending a castle could easily maintain a brazier, this would not have been possible for a more mobile handgonner moving around the field of battle in the 14th century. Furthermore, tests done by the Swiss re-enactor Ulrich Bretscher have shown that using a hot wire to light a handgonne results in the wire getting bent by the recoil. The handgonner would have had to straighten out a red-hot poker in the midst of battle every time he fired his weapon, or have kept several pokers in a brazier that he would have had to move around. Logic dictates that slow matches, or some other unknown form of ignition, did exist before the 15th century. The straight black lines shown on many of the manuscript illustrations do not necessarily indicate a wire; they are simply too small to show any sort of detail. Significantly, braziers and open fires are rarely shown next to handgonners, although several records mention them as part of the equipment sent along with the artillery. Even Milemete's two illustrations of a pot de fer, dating all the way back to 1326, show not a hot wire, but a thin, curved object held on the end of a pole. This could very well have been a slow match.

SPREAD

After their appearance in the early 14th century, black powder weapons spread quickly until by the end of that century they could be found throughout Europe.

A Swedish wall painting from the second half of the 15th century showing 'The Death of St Olaf'. A handgonner with a simple socketed weapon can be seen on the left. That such a crude piece would be used at this late period is not due to Sweden being a peripheral area; it was not. There are also late 15th-century French and German illustrations showing 'early' handgonne forms.

Cannon spread more quickly than handgonnes because of their usefulness in sieges, and *castellans* (governors of castles) were quick to adopt them for defensive purposes. A chronicle written *c.*1381 in Brittany mentions 'saltpetre, charcoal, and new sulphur, placed in every castle'. Black powder weapons became symbols of power. At his coronation in 1397, King Erik of Denmark, Sweden, and Norway impressed the assembled nobles by firing off several *bössor* (smaller cannon often used in the defence of ships and castles). Even at this late date some of the more rural aristocracy had probably never seen a cannon fired, and certainly not the medieval equivalent of a 21-gun salute. It is interesting to note that the bössor crews were mostly German, the more southern peoples still having an edge in black powder technology.

Poland obtained handgonnes fairly early, the first reference being from 1383. Many were of the socketed cast bronze variety with multifaceted barrels and hook. However, they did not appear in large numbers until the mid-15th century, a period in which Polish artillery saw rapid advancement. This was a time of struggle with the Teutonic Knights, when the country needed every tool at its disposal to combat a strong and determined enemy.

Black powder weapons spread as far as Russia by the late 14th century. While Russia may have benefited from its geographical proximity to the Chinese and Mongols, which would have led to an early familiarity with gunpowder, the surviving handgonnes are European in style. The first mention of the weapon in the region is in a vague reference from 1376 of a device firing from the walls of a Bulgar city on the river Volga against Russian attackers. A more specific reference comes from 1382, when cannons and *tyufyaki* (a type of handgonne, plural of *tyufyak*) were used to defend the walls of Moscow. The tyufyak was a heavy handgonne. A later book dated to the 17th century called *The Cannons and Arquebuses Description Book* mentions tyufyaki with calibres of 40–85mm. The cannon used in this fight was of the old type, firing a bolt instead of a ball, yet its crew was skilled or lucky enough to hit a Tatar prince. Gun foundries appeared in Russia in the late 15th century.

The arquebus was mentioned in Russia from 1408 onwards, and at that stage the term almost certainly referred to a hackbut and not a proper matchlock. The arquebus did not become commonplace until the 1470s when it replaced the tyufyak in the field. The older, heavier weapon was still used to defend fortified positions, where its lower mobility was not such an issue. By the end of the century there were several types of handgonne in use in Russia. Besides the two previously mentioned, there was the *samopal*, which appears to have been a smaller handgonne, and the *ruchnitsa*, a long-barrelled musket. Chroniclers report that one of the main advantages of handgonnes was that they caused panic in the ranks of the Tatars, the Russians' worst enemy. Often a volley would send the Tatars running before they even had a chance to close. The handgonne's greatest victory came in 1480 at the river Ugra, where the Muscovites arrayed a large number of cannon and arquebuses and drove the Tatars off the river bank, forcing an early end to their planned invasion. This battle was the first step in overthrowing Tatar domination over Russia. Handgonnes had become so effective that the last mention of the crossbow being used as a weapon of war in Russia was in 1486.

The spread of the handgonne must be seen in the larger context of what some researchers have called the 'Infantry Revolution' of the late 14th and 15th centuries. The heavily armoured knights that had dominated the battlefield in earlier times were replaced by organized infantry armed with pikes, polearms, bows and crossbows. All of these weapons could defeat a knight if used properly, preferably in tandem with a large group of similarly armed troops. An archer or pikeman was cheaper to hire, train and equip than a knight, and could therefore be used in greater numbers. In battle after battle, groups of determined infantry defeated heavily armoured cavalry.

Handgonners fitted perfectly into this development. They needed little training and their equipment cost far less than that of a knight. What the gonners may have lacked in individual effectiveness was made up for in numbers. An 'Artillery Revolution' was happening at the same time, defeating castles and walled towns with the same ruthless efficiency as infantry were defeating knights, so further elevating the status of black powder weapons.

THE HUSSITE WARS

Handgonnes truly came into their own during the Hussite Wars in Bohemia from 1419 to 1436. The Bohemian church reformer Jan Hus led a protest movement against the sale of indulgences and other corrupt practices by the church elite. When he was assassinated in 1415, while attending what was supposed to be a conciliatory church council, his supporters rose up in revolt against the Holy Roman Empire and the Church itself. Their rebellion became an assertion of Czech national identity against the ruling Germans. They called themselves Hussites after their slain leader and rallied around Jan Zizka, a one-eyed knight who had fought for the Polish against the Teutonic Knights.

Jan Zizka knew his eager peasants stood little chance against knights in the open field, so he used their limited resources to full advantage. He converted farm wagons into mobile forts by covering them with wooden planks and chaining them together. These wagons could be drawn into a square or circle called a *wagenburg*.

The origins of the wagenburg are unclear. Wagons sometimes acted as barriers in medieval warfare, especially when the enemy came upon an army on the march, such as at the Battle of the Herrings in 1429, where the English lined up a supply column of carts carrying salted fish as a protection against a French attack. In Western Europe the use of wagons was generally a spur-of-the-moment affair; in Eastern Europe it became a part of battlefield tactics. It is possible Zizka learned this tactic during his service in Eastern Europe, as it is similar to a Russian tactic used against Tatar and Polish cavalry, and by the Lithuanians against the Teutonic Knights, but he could have developed it independently.

Each wagon was fortified by wooden siding equipped with loopholes. Another flap covered the bottom portion so attackers couldn't crawl underneath. Detailed lists of equipment show Zizka's talent for organization. Individual carts came with two axes, two spades, two pickaxes, two hoes, two shovels, lances with hooks, and a chain with a hook to attach the wagon to the next one in the formation. The tools were for adding entrenchments if the wagenburg stayed in the same position for any long period of time.

Although reports vary and numbers probably changed according to circumstance, every wagon had a crew of perhaps ten or 20 men. One account states that a wagon would have two drivers, two handgonners, six crossbowmen, 14 men armed with *flails* (a simple adaptation of the common threshing flail), four men with *halberds* (long polearms equipped with a heavy blade, end spike and pick), and two men carrying pavises.

The crossbowmen and handgonners kept up a steady fire from the loopholes. The men with flails and halberds protected the gaps between the wagons while being covered by the *pavisiers* (pavise carriers). Thus the enemy would face a solid wall of wood bristling with weapons.

Much of the wagenburg equipment could be found or easily made in any peasant village. The tools and flails were everyday items. A blacksmith could make a halberd or simply adapt a farm implement and put it on the end of a pole. He could also make the basic handgonnes of the time. Only crossbows were somewhat more complicated to make, although easier to learn how to use than a longbow. The wagons, of course, were common farm carts adapted with basic carpentry skills.

The emphasis was on rate of fire. With eight soldiers having ranged weapons in each wagon, they could maintain devastating volleys or a continuous fire. Some would crawl under the cart and fire from loopholes cut through the bottom flap. The wagons even contained a supply of rocks so that those not armed with a ranged weapon could throw them at the enemy while their comrades reloaded. Some carts had cannons mounted on them.

Zizka first tried his wagenburg tactics at the small battle of Sudomer on 25 March 1420. This victory strengthened the Hussite cause and proved the effectiveness of the new strategy. Zizka must have certainly been impressed with the performance of his handgonners outside the city of Kutna Hora on 21 December 1421. He was isolated in his wagon fortress on the hill overlooking the town and surrounded by Royalist

A contemporary illustration of a Hussite wagenburg. Four wagons are drawn together around a camp. The Hussites are using a variety of weapons such as handgonnes, crossbows and flails. One is even throwing a rock. (Austrian National Library, Vienna, Picture Archive, Cod. MS 3069, f.38v)

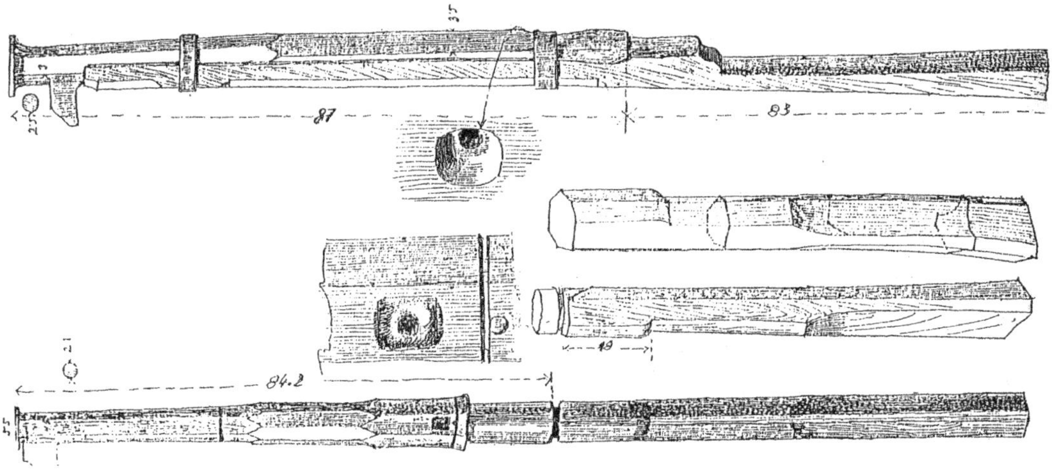

A pair of Hussite hackbuts, seen from the left (upper example) and top (lower example). The upper gonne has a carefully shaped stock, while the lower one shows some detailed casting. Both are about 1,700mm long. The upper gonne has a 25mm calibre.

crusaders, who outnumbered him yet couldn't take his position. In the meantime another portion of the Royalist army worked their way around the Hussite position, burst into town, and started slaughtering the citizens. Zizka saw the town was lost and that he could not hold his position for ever, so he ordered his handgonners and light artillery to concentrate their fire on one part of the line. They broke through, and the Hussites survived to fight another day thanks to what may have been the first tactical use of concentrated handgonne fire.

Handgonnes worked well in this type of warfare. They could be rested on the lip of the loophole for better aim, and the gonner remained protected while he went through the slow task of reloading. They proved so effective that when Zizka reorganized his army between 1421 and 1427 he increased the number of handgonnes. Several Bohemian cities and towns had rallied under his banner and with their production facilities he could deploy many more black powder weapons than before.

The use of the wagenburg was essentially a defensive tactic. The enemy would attack but the heavy fire from the wagons would disorganize their ranks. Then part of the wagenburg would open up and the Hussites would counterattack with infantry and the small number of knights and armoured cavalry at their disposal. The Hussites even took the war to the enemy by invading hostile neighbours such as Hungary and Bavaria, and the wagenburg would be brought along as a system of offensive defence. By bringing these monstrosities into an adversary's province and looting the countryside, the enemy could usually be goaded into making an attack. The knights fell for this tactic again and again, convinced of their superiority over 'peasant rabble'. Eventually, however, they began to learn from their experience and defeated some Hussite armies by luring them out of their protection with fake retreats or by destroying the wagons with concentrated artillery fire.

The wagenburg tactic proved highly effective, and the eventual failure of the Hussite movement was due more to internal dissent than outside pressure. Other armies began to adopt the wagenburg but advances in artillery, with armies replacing the cumbersome early cannon with more mobile and accurate weapons, eventually made the wagenburg obsolete.

The success of the Hussites made other rulers take notice. In 1421, Duke Albrecht V, Archduke of Austria, whose lands had been devastated by the Hussites, called for a muster of one man from every ten households. He stipulated that out of every 20 recruits, three should have handgonnes and eight should have crossbows. The rest should have pikes or flails. Significantly, each group of 20 men should also have a wagon.

Leaders increased the use of artillery in response to the Hussite Wars. The Holy Roman Emperor insisted his subjects increase their stock of cannon and handgonnes. For example, in an ordinance dated 1427, Nuremberg had to supply 'a large stonegun, that shoots 2cwt', six smaller stoneguns, 12 palisade guns, and 60 handgonnes, as well as six master gunners. A generation later at the battle of Pillenreuth, 11 March 1450, the Nurembergers were instructed by their Swiss officer, Henry of Malters, to arm themselves with a crossbow, handgonne, or halberd.

An account from 1431 tells of the army of Regensburg leaving their town to join with other troops to fight the Hussites. The 248 men included 16 handgonners and 71 crossbowmen. This little force had six cannon, 3cwt of cannon balls, and 2cwt of lead shot, the last presumably for the handgonnes although some might have been reserved for grapeshot in the cannon. Such a large amount of shot indicates that the handgonners expected to see lots of duty. That even so small a band had such a large number of black powder weapons also shows how common such weaponry had become. An interesting note says that among the equipment in the supply wagons there were 19 handgonnes. It is not clear if these are extra to those carried by the 16 handgonners or not.

THE WARS OF THE ROSES

The wagenburg was the most famous tactic heightening the effectiveness of the handgonne, but not the only one. Clever commanders tried various means to keep the enemy far enough away that they could not hurt the handgonners, but were close enough to be shot. The second battle of St Albans on 17 February 1461 during the Wars of the Roses is one such example.

The Yorkists held the important city of St Albans north of London and knew the Lancastrian army was close by. They expected the Lancastrians to approach the city from the north, so they prepared an elaborate defence in depth by deploying their troops behind a series of hedges and spreading out a long band of *caltrops* (spiked iron balls). Behind these, at any paths or gaps through the hedges, the Yorkists set up large nets – 7.3m (24ft) long and 1.2m (4ft) wide, with spikes at the intersections. These nets were commonly used aboard ships to stop boarding parties, and the Yorkists hoped that combined with the caltrops they would slow or stop all but a determined infantry advance. No cavalry charge would be able to force its way through.

Behind this fortification the Yorkists lined up archers, crossbowmen, Burgundian mercenary handgonners, and artillery. The Lancastrians would be cut to pieces before they could make their way through the protection. It was one of the most formidable systems of defence ever set up by a medieval army in the field, but it was doomed to fail. The Lancastrians made a forced march and came on St Albans from another direction altogether, quickly taking the town and forcing the Yorkist army to turn and fight from an unprotected flank. The short, bloody battle resulted in a complete victory for the Lancastrians.

According to William Gregory's *Great Chronicle of London*, 'before the gunners and Burgundians could level their guns they were busily fighting'. This seems to indicate that both the artillery and the handgonners were unable to fire in time. Perhaps since the attack came as a complete surprise the handgonners had not yet loaded their guns, and

The wagenburg (previous pages)

From 1419 to 1436 the Hussite movement of Bohemia fought for political and religious independence from the Holy Roman Empire. This mostly peasant army held their own against knights and armoured infantry by fighting from protective circles of armoured wagons. Here we see part of a Hussite wagenburg, a circle of wagons drawn up for battle. Wagon A on the lower left shows how an attacking force would have seen it. Note the row of handgonners and crossbowmen inside, and the pavise with handgonners on the far left. Attackers received a constant fire and would have had trouble retaliating against the well-protected Hussites.

Wagon B is attached to Wagon A by a chain and a hook, a simple way of keeping the wagenburg together. From this angle we can see inside the wagon. A row of handgonners and crossbowmen are firing while a group of their comrades stand behind them reloading. Note that Wagons A and B are of slightly different construction. Wagon B is simpler, with a series of planks roped together and thrown over the side for added protection. A more elaborate and effective defence can be seen in Wagon A, where the side rises up and is equipped with loopholes for firing.

The spaces between wagons were blocked with pavises, large shields set into the ground with a bottom spike and a supporting rod. The pavise between Wagons B and C is manned by a two-man crew firing a trestle gun, a small mobile cannon that proved quite effective against infantry. One of the crew lights the charge with a slow match while the other leans against the gun with his full weight to absorb the recoil. On the rear of the trestle gun note the arc pierced with a series of holes through which a pin is fixed to adjust the elevation. In front of Wagon B, a woman with a pitchfork has managed to hook a knight and is pulling him off his horse while her male comrade hits him with a flail. There are numerous references to Hussite women fighting alongside men. The Hussites' simple weapons, altered from farm implements, proved easy to make and deadly in action. Wagon C is seen from behind and shows the opening through which fighters could enter and leave the wagon. Wagon C and the pavise to the left of it are manned by handgonners and crossbowmen.

Within the circle of wagons various Hussites are either reloading their handgonnes and crossbows, or waiting with their flails, spears, and polearms for a chance to strike. Others take care of the draft horses that would pull the wagons on the march. Still others tend the wounded. The armoured rider in the centre is one of a small number of Hussite minor nobility. He is observing the battle and waiting until the attacking force is disorganized and dispirited, at which point he will signal for the wagenburg to open so his fellow knights can charge out in a counterattack.

A well-made bronze hook gun, European, *c.*1500. (Courtesy Royal Armouries)

lacked the time to do so before the Lancastrians closed and engaged them in hand-to-hand combat. It is also possible that Gregory meant only that the artillery did not get a chance to turn and find new range (what he means by 'level') before the Lancastrians were upon them.

Gregory also made some interesting comments about the Burgundian weapons: 'The Burgundians had such instruments that would shoot both pellets of lead and arrows of an ell in length with six feathers, three in the middle and three at one end, with a very big head of iron on the other end, and wild fire, all together.'

Once again Gregory's account is unclear. While the detailed description of the arrows suggests personal observation, an *ell* is 1.14m (45in). It is unlikely such a long arrow would have been fired from a handgonne. There is no other evidence for such a weapon. More likely he confused the handgonne ammunition – the pellets of lead he mentions – with long arrows used in cannons. It is interesting to see gun arrows like those of the old pot de fer at this late date. The 'wild fire' he mentions is probably a *petard*, a ceramic jar filled with explosive and thrown like a crude grenade. While Gregory's account of the battle is at times detailed, it is a perfect example of the confusion contemporary chroniclers had when discussing unfamiliar weapons. At that time handgonnes and artillery had been in England for more than a century, yet they could still cause vagueness and uncertainty among educated observers.

Ten years later the Yorkists and Lancastrians were still fighting, and using increasing numbers of handgonnes. King Edward IV of the House of York had Flemish handgonners on his side. The *Great Chronicle of London* describes these foreign handgonners as 'sooty', presumably a description of their clothes, hands, and faces grimy from the flash of the priming powder. Edward entered London on 11 April 1471 and the chronicle says he had 500 'black and smoky sort of Flemish gunners' marching at the head of his army. His army has been estimated at 5,000–6,000 men, so handgonners comprised a sizeable minority.

In both battles of this campaign, Edward started with a bombardment of the Lancastrian foe. At the battle of Barnet on 14 April 1471, hostilities commenced at about 7.00am in a thick fog. Both sides opened up with artillery, handgonnes, and archers. Edward had more black powder weapons than the Lancastrians but casualties seem to have been roughly equal and thus cancelled each other out. Edward soon decided to close with his enemy. At the battle of Tewkesbury on 4 May 1471 the Lancastrians were once again weaker in ordnance, and so Edward's Yorkist army again opened up with a bombardment. Edward had several field cannon, as well as archers and presumably handgonners, although they are not specifically mentioned. They fired at the extreme bowshot range of 275m. One wonders if the handgonners could have hit anything at such a distance, but the added smoke and fire would have at least had an effect on morale. As a further possible advantage, Edward's artillery may have been supplied with canister shot, since this was known in Germany from about 1400. The Lancastrians had less artillery and perhaps fewer archers and handgonners. They suffered the worst of this long-range duel and decided to advance. In both cases the initial bombardment did not decide the battle, but it forced one side or the other to make a move.

THE LATE 15TH CENTURY

By the second half of the 15th century handgonnes had become commonplace. They could be found in considerable numbers in most, if not all, European armies alongside bows and crossbows.

This period also saw a centralization of gunpowder technology. Kings and princes gained a greater control of taxation, especially in Germany, and used their wealth to buy black powder weapons in superior numbers and quality to outpace the military development of their weaker neighbours and the lesser nobility. This lopsided arms race helped further centralize authority and encouraged the development of nation states.

Cities became more important as trade and industry grew. The industrial towns of the Low Countries became major centres of production. Blast furnaces, essential to the production of cheap, high-quality iron, and which had first developed in Belgium by 1340, spread throughout the Low Countries by the first quarter of the 15th century. This region became the centre of European cannon production, and the large numbers of handgonnes from the same area shows that the infantry weapon benefited from industrial growth too.

In Italy, Milan and Venice grew tired of the unreliable and expensive *condottierre* mercenaries and created a system of *provisionati*, trained urban militia available at all times to defend their homeland. These included a large proportion of handgonners, with weapons supplied by the towns' workhouses. At the beginning of the War of Ferrara in 1482, the Milanese fielded 1,250 handgonners and only 233 crossbowmen. This force also included 352 arquebusiers, who used a far more effective firearm with a spring-loaded trigger activated by a button, demonstrating the old handgonne and the more developed (and no doubt more expensive) arquebus being used side by side. While specific mention of this is rare in the chronicles, it was likely to have been quite a common occurrence during the transition period of the latter half of the 15th century.

The Swiss became great champions of the handgonne. Given that they served as mercenaries the length and breadth of Europe, they were in a position to learn (and teach) the effectiveness of the developing weapon. The muster roll for the canton of Zurich in 1443 shows that out of 2,760 men, only 61 (2 per cent) carried handgonnes. In contrast, crossbowmen numbered 473 (17 per cent), while 635 (23 per cent) carried pikes, and the remaining 1,591 (58 per cent) carried halberds and axes. By the Burgundian

OPPOSITE
Arquebusiers on boats firing at opponents on land and water. By the late 15th century, handgonners were comfortable fighting in a variety of conditions. From the Swiss *Amtliche Berner Chronik* of 1483, by Diebold Schilling. (Burgerbibliothek Bern, Mss.h.h.I.1, p.621)

Die von Bernn, Friburg, Solottern und
Biell lagen mit iren paneri vñ mac-
ten zů Murten und da umb und ware
gantz gerüst und giengen tag und nacht zů samen
raten wie si die iren erlösen und entschütten möchte
und waren alweg des willens von statt zů ziehe
da kament an ein andern botten und briefe von den
eidgnon und andern verwanten man solt sich
enthalten und niendert hin ziehen noch ufbrechen

Iron handgonne found near the battlefield of Grandson, 1476. It has a flared muzzle with reinforcing wire behind it. The bulge in the centre of the barrel is due to its having burst. Several burst handgonnes have been found, often in the moats of castles where they had been discarded. (Foundation for Art, Culture and History, Castle of Grandson)

Wars of 1474–7, the numbers of crossbowmen and handgonners had become roughly equal. In battle the handgonners often acted as skirmishers or a mobile reserve. They tended to be lightly armoured and therefore faster moving than their targets. Indeed one can imagine them rushing close to a ponderous formation of pikemen or heavy infantry, firing their weapons, then hurrying away to reload before rushing in again. The 1443 Zurich muster roll mentions that a mixture of crossbowmen and handgonners went in front of the vanguard and behind the rearguard, probably to act as skirmishers to delay the enemy until the pikemen in the centre could get ready, or to disrupt the enemy line to soften it up for an attack.

At the battle of Grandson on 2 March 1476, the Swiss handgonners moved ahead of the main army to fight Charles the Bold's men as skirmishers. Later in the battle they went forward with some crossbowmen and together they fired on the Burgundians. At another point they got into hand-to-hand combat with the Burgundian knights. While this was certainly not their preferred method of fighting, they acquitted themselves well, showing they were trained with hand-to-hand weapons. In all probability they would have been able to fire off a few deadly shots at point-blank range. They fought so actively in this battle that by its peak they had run out of most of their shot.

Handgonners had a special place at the battle of Nancy on 5 January 1477, where 800 of them served as a mobile unit to assist either the van or the centre. Handgonners also served in the main columns of both sides. The Swiss attack on the Burgundian left flank was composed of a wedge formation of pikemen supported only by handgonners. While a mixture of crossbowmen and handgonners usually supported the pikes, this instance shows the Swiss commanders had confidence that handgonners could do the job alone.

Although the Burgundians came to grief at the hands of the Swiss, they had one of the most advanced armies in Europe and arguably the most advanced black powder weaponry. Their extensive, mobile, and modern artillery train is outside the scope of this volume, but proved its worth again and again in the field. Handgonnes too acted as an important part of their force. John the Fearless, Duke of Burgundy, had at least 4,000 handgonners in his army by 1411. When his successor Philip the Good planned a crusade against the Turks in 1456, he included 500–600 handgonners in the roster, commanded by a master of artillery. They were to be equal in number to the traditional backbone of the medieval army, the cavalry. In a muster on 20 May 1471, Charles the Bold called for

Swivel gun, 16th or 17th century, from the Low Countries. Swivel guns were popular on ships, and were essentially oversized handgonnes. Hand-lit versions of the swivel gun continued to be used well after the matchlock had become common. This example was dredged up from the Rijn/Waal near Dorestad, now Wijk bij Duurstede. (Legermuseum, Delft)

Danish handgonne, *c.*1500. There is a hook clamped near the reinforced muzzle, and the slots in the wooden stock suggest this may once have had a lock. There is a pan for the touch-hole and small front and rear sights. Length 1,370mm, calibre 32mm, weight 17.25kg. (Danish National Museum of Military History)

reinforcements of 1,200 crossbowmen, 1,250 handgonners and 1,250 pikemen. Another document from the same year shows crossbowmen and handgonners were not only equal in numbers, but they received the same pay. Some 15th-century French and Burgundian accounts mention handgonners being paid more than cavalrymen.

The Ordinance of Bohain-en-Vermandois (France) on 13 November 1472 summoned 1,200 men-at-arms, each accompanied by a mounted page and a swordsman, 3,000 mounted archers, 600 mounted crossbowmen, 2,000 pikemen, 1,000 archers, and 600 handgonners. It required each handgonner to wear a sleeved mail shirt, a *gorgerin* (armour protecting the throat and neck and made of mail or plate), a *sallet* (a type of helmet), and a breastplate. He also had to carry a dagger and sword. This rare glimpse into the equipment of handgonners makes it clear they were not considered poor cousins to the other types of fighter. Their armour and hand-to-hand weapons allowed them to fight as regular infantry when the occasion arose. While they tried to keep at a distance from the enemy, there would inevitably be times when this equipment would be necessary. The Ordinance does not mention any leg armour, and many of the period illustrations show handgonners without any such protection. It may be that handgonners preferred their legs to be unencumbered so that they could move around more freely as skirmishers.

Like the Swiss, the Italians used mounted crossbowmen and handgonners for scouting, foraging, skirmishing, and pursuing a fleeing enemy. Some intriguing images from this period show well-armoured knights firing a handgonne while mounted. The crossbowmen and handgonners were probably not so well armoured, and may have dismounted to fight, although there are depictions of them firing from horseback. By 1490 the Papal States had mounted infantrymen armed with arquebuses.

Another innovation in the second half of the 15th century was the pre-measured charge that could be poured into the handgonne, which greatly speeded up loading. It is unclear when it first came into use, and may have been practised in some areas a few decades earlier, but it was certainly common by the century's end.

By the middle of the 15th century black powder weapons had become widespread on ships (there is even evidence of their use in the 14th century). In addition to handgonnes, ships were equipped with cannons and/or swivel guns. Naval artillery were breech-loading pieces that tended to be smaller and more standardized than their counterparts on land. Captains tried to equip their ships with cannon of the same barrel length, calibre, and chamber size. Contemporary sources show them being used in both ship-to-ship combat and against targets on land.

Thus by the end of the 15th century the handgonne had developed into an effective weapon able to be used in attack and defence, on foot or mounted, on land or at sea, and as its accuracy and dependability increased it took prime place among the ranged infantry weapons of European arsenals. Cheaper and more powerful gunpowder, plus a more efficient shape and better dimensions, created an affordable and deadly weapon. What had started out as a crude device best kept in a fortified position where the powder could be kept functioning and where the handgonner had a convenient wall on which to brace, had now become a viable weapon in the field.

THE DEVELOPMENT OF THE MATCHLOCK

As the chronicles are somewhat vague regarding arquebuses in the latter half of the 15th century, it is difficult to determine whether they refer to pre-matchlock, serpentine, or button-lock weapons. While there are depictions of serpentine matchlocks dating to as early as 1411, handgonnes that were fired by simply touching a slow match to the priming powder remained in use until the end of the 15th century and even beyond.

One type of handgonne that survived the spread of the matchlock for a time was what was often called the *hook* gun. This was essentially an oversized combination of the hackbut and arquebus. Illustrations dating to 1502 of the arsenal of King Maximilian of Hapsburg (later Holy Roman Emperor) show the weapon to be quite large, about 1,525mm (60in) long. It had a hook either cast into the barrel or as a wooden attachment to the stock, which could be lodged on the edge of a parapet or on a wooden tripod. The gun was fired by a slow match held in the hand, and its size was such that shoulder or hip firing was impossible, and thus the need for a lock was less important. The hook gun saw service throughout the early 16th century, long after other pre-matchlock firearms had fallen out of favour. Its large size made it a fearsome weapon and still useful despite what must have been a slow firing speed and the need for two or three men to carry all the equipment. With soldiers wearing lighter armour by this time, a hook gun firing into close ranks may have cut through more than one target.

Despite this one exception, and a few primitive specimens still found in backward areas, by the early 1500s the days of the pre-matchlock handgonne were basically over.

TOP
A close-up of the lock and touch-hole of the serpentine matchlock below. The touch-hole is a simple affair without a proper pan. A maker's mark and sight are on the top of the barrel near the touch-hole. (Croatian History Museum)

BOTTOM
A simple serpentine matchlock from Croatia. Part of the lock mechanism is apparently missing, as can be seen from the holes near the lock. It was found in a cave by the river Kupa, near Brlog in Karlovac region. It is dated by the museum to the early 16th century, but is perhaps earlier. Length 1,240mm, calibre 35mm, weight 10.6kg. (Croatian History Museum)

AIMING

One matter of great debate among historians and re-enactors is just how to aim a handgonne properly. Various methods appear in period illustrations, including holding the handgonne under the armpit, against the hip, against the shoulder, over the shoulder, or against the ground. Sometimes an assistant lights the priming powder so the handgonner can hold on with both hands, but mostly the handgonner is shown aiming and firing unaided.

This creates an obvious problem and it is difficult to see how a gonner could have kept an eye on the target while trying to place the match into the priming powder. There is no good solution for this, although re-enactors have found the best method is to clench the handgonne under the armpit while aiming with that hand, and lighting the priming with the other. Aim is done more by 'feel' than actual sighting. As already noted, accuracy was not such an issue when shooting at a mass of men as it was simply a matter of making sure the ball shot out reasonably level. However, there are many depictions of handgonners firing at individuals during sieges, where accuracy would be vital. It is impossible to gauge just how accurate a handgonne could be in such circumstances, but handgonners are likely to have had a fair amount of practice. Additionally, they would have had knowledge of their particular weapon's peculiarities, such as shooting a bit low and to the right, and would have compensated for this while aiming.

A rack of four heavy hook guns from the late 15th/early 16th century. Measurements are given for all four from the top gun to the bottom. Total length 1,515mm, barrel length 920mm, calibre 25.5mm. Total length 1,510mm, barrel length 885mm, calibre 25mm. Total length 1,433mm, barrel length 908mm, calibre 19mm. Total length 1,838mm, barrel length 1,255mm, calibre 26.5mm. (Bayerisches Armeemuseum)

FIRING A HACKBUT

This series of photos shows the firing sequence for a replica hackbut, based on an example of *c.*1420–1440 from the Burgundian army. It is an .80-calibre weapon with no lock. The photoshoot is courtesy of the Company of the Wolfe Argent, a group in the United States that re-enacts soldiers from the army of Charles the Bold, Duke of Burgundy. Bob Reed organized the photoshoot, photos are by Jennifer L. R. Reed, the handgonner is J. Morgan Kuberry, and the 'candle safe' (the man with the lantern) is Phil Dickson.

1. The handgonner takes a bullet from his pouch.
2. Measuring powder from the powder horn. In the days before prepared cartridges, this was done by eye. Any experienced handgonner would be able to do this, but with the variable quality of gunpowder in that period there would always be a certain amount of guesswork.
3. The bullet and powder. Note that original bullets would have been lead, not stainless steel like those preferred by modern re-enactors.
4. Pouring the charge into the barrel.
5. Ramming the charge home with a ramrod.
6. Stowing the ramrod. Note that at this early date handgonnes did not include a holder beneath the barrel for the ramrod, and the gonner simply stuck the ramrod through his belt.
7. Priming the pan. This has to be done carefully. Too little powder and the charge may not ignite. Too much and the pan and vent

could get fouled, and the extra sparks can be hazardous.

8. Lighting the match by holding it up to the flame of a covered lantern. Various methods could be used to light the match, all of them inconvenient for soldiers in the field. It is not known for certain how the match was generally lit, but the large numbers of lanterns listed among the artillery equipment for the Burgundian army suggests that this method was the correct one.

9. Blowing on the match.

10. Getting ready to fire. Note that the gonner keeps his weapon well away from his face.

11. Firing the handgonne.

Danish handgonne of brass, *c.*1500. This elaborately made example, one of the finest surviving, has front and rear sights. Length 929mm, calibre 24.1mm, weight 17.69kg. (Danish National Museum of Military History)

INCENDIARY DEVICES AND EXPLOSIVES

A word should be said about other hand-held black powder weapons. While the handgonne became the favoured black powder infantry weapon, soldiers also used incendiary devices from the very beginning of the black powder weapons period.

The *fire lance* or *fire tube* appeared before the handgonne in China and was also known in Europe. For the European weapon there is a detailed description in Biringuccio's 1540 manual *Pirotechnia*. While this is somewhat later than the period covered in this book, such weapons from the 15th century were probably the same or similar. Biringuccio observed that the tubes were made of wood, iron, or sheet copper and measured about a metre long and with a calibre of about 30mm. The tube was filled with gunpowder alternated with balls filled with gunpowder and coated in pine resin, sulphur, and gunpowder. This tube was then fixed to the end of a long pole and lit at the rear with a fuse or priming powder.

These fire tubes shot out a spray of sparks and flame punctuated by flaming balls, much like an oversized version of a modern Roman candle. Its effect on a group of massed men or a village of thatch huts would have been considerable. The tubes never achieved the popularity of the handgonne, probably because they lacked the handgonne's penetrative power. While they appeared to be fearsome weapons, a well-armoured man had little to fear from them, and once soldiers became accustomed to their pyrotechnics they lost much of their ability to demoralize the enemy. Yet they did have their uses against lightly armoured or poorly disciplined men and flammable structures.

Other weapons using gunpowder included *fire arrows* and grenades. Fire arrows became common in the 15th century and lasted into the 17th century. Manuscript illustrations often show them being used in sieges in conjunction with regular arrows, handgonnes and artillery. To make a fire arrow the archer attached a small pouch to the front of an arrow containing, according to recipes of the day, various proportions of saltpetre, sulphur, and other ingredients (one recipe calls for gunpowder alone). The pouch would then be lit and the arrow fired. Insufficient research has been done on these devices to determine how the pouch managed not to explode or burn up before reaching its target.

Grenades were simple weapons to create. As early as the 1260s Bacon had theorized in his *Opus Tertium* that the firecracker could be turned into a weapon by encasing the gunpowder in a solid material. Early grenades were often ceramic jars filled with gunpowder. Larger specimens, sometimes called petards, could even blow open a city gate if set correctly.

A 19th-century reconstruction of a gonner firing his weapon. The handgonne is held tightly under the arm while it is lit with a slow match.

IMPACT

A turning point in history

THE STATUS OF THE GONNER

There is a common misperception that medieval people looked on black powder weapons and their wielders as something diabolical, to be loathed and feared. This, like the idea that early gonnes were ineffective and dangerous to use, is more exaggeration than truth. The fact that black powder weapons spread so quickly and universally refutes it.

While the 13th-century writers spoke of gunpowder in almost mystical terms, sometimes even putting their recipes in code, by the 14th century the recipe books were common in number and routine in tone. Occasionally one finds a critical note, such as John of Mirfield's description of gunpowder in *c.*1400 as 'for that devilish instrument of war colloquially termed gunne'. Devilish it may have been, but that did not stop John from providing a recipe. It should also be noted that black powder weapons were never prohibited, like the crossbow is said to have been in the famous Second Lateran Council in 1139 (although some scholars have disputed there ever was such a ban).

Although there are a couple of references to captured gonners being put to death, this need not mean they were thought of as diabolical. They were specialized soldiers, especially the artillerists, and to kill them ensured they could never again serve the enemy. It was their practical value, not any moral judgement, that led to their deaths.

Indeed, black powder weapons were considered objects of pride, especially the large cannon. They were shown off at major state functions, given pet names, painted onto banners, and boasted about by their owners. The aristocracy of Europe saw nothing 'devilish' about them.

OPPOSITE
An army on the march. The arquebusiers carry their weapons reversed. One in the centre carries a match in one hand and his powder horn is slung over the butt of his weapon. Note the hole in the butt of each arquebus. Its purpose is unclear; two theories are that it was either to hang the weapon from a wall during storage, or to hold the match. From the Swiss *Amtliche Berner Chronik* of 1483, by Diebold Schilling. (Burgerbibliothek Bern, Mss.h.h.I.1, p.43)

In dem vorgenanten zinstag nach mitten tag
do kament die von Glarus mit ir paner und
einem schönen zuge darzu die im Gastel mit
ir paner und gantzer macht zu denen von Switz uff
den Etzel und seiten die von Glarus denen von Zurich
ab dem weg einen brieff und hies man die im Gastel
widder zu denen von Zurich ziehen

Achtung ...!

OPPOSITE

An army attacking a fortified town. The armoured arquebusier on the left holds his weapon reversed and it seems to be equipped with a serpentine lock. The arquebusier on the right is using a ramrod to load his weapon. It too appears to have a serpentine, although it is very faint in this image. A satchel for shot lies at his feet. From the Swiss *Amtliche Berner Chronik* of 1483, by Diebold Schilling. (Burgerbibliothek Bern, Mss.h.h.I.1, p.88)

ADDITIONAL DUTIES OF THE GONNER

As already seen, the gonner soon became incorporated into European armies. The artillery provided a valuable asset while the handgonners supplemented existing contingents of archers or crossbowmen. As the wielders of a new and specialized weapon, their responsibilities went beyond simply using it in battle; gonners were expected to maintain and fix their weapons and also deal with gunpowder.

Contemporary sources say little about the providers of gunpowder. In some cases the same person supplied the materials and mixed them, such as the Burgundian master of artillery Jean des Roches, who wrote down his recipe for gunpowder in 1413. In 1418 William Wodeward supplied the English army only with the raw materials for powder as well as the metal for black powder weapons. Other individuals are noted as having made both gonnes and powder, or having acted as teachers to train others, but a survey of the sources reveals no hard-and-fast rule. The role of the supplier appears to have varied depending on skill and the needs of the consumer at the moment.

More often than not the gonners themselves mixed the ingredients to make gunpowder, and there are numerous references to sulphur and saltpetre being shipped separately; as already noted, in the days before corning this was necessary because the ingredients could separate. In 1378 the Duke of Brittany sent mixed gunpowder to the siege of Brest; he also sent along a mortar and pestle 'to make gunpowder', or perhaps remix it. Even as late as 1475, well into the corning era, Edward IV's master of artillery in France, William Roos, received a shipment of ten barrels of gunpowder as well as considerable supplies of unbroken brimstone, saltpetre that had been sieved so as to be ready to mix, and charcoal. Of the 14 records from the town of Rennes dating from 1420 to 1491, only three mention the powder being fully mixed and ready to use, despite the fact that a German expert had been imported to teach the townspeople how to make it. Apparently military leaders still worried about imperfectly made gunpowder spoiling or separating in transit. Thus it was left to the gonners to mix the powder in the field shortly before use.

HOW EFFECTIVE WERE HANDGONNES?

The major question regarding handgonnes is how effective they actually were. Contemporary sources tend to be vague, and every modern test falls short of complete authenticity, but there is enough data to create a general picture of the capabilities of the pre-matchlock handgonne.

The question then raises a counterquestion – effective compared with what? There is considerable debate in scholarly and re-enactment circles as to the penetrative power of arrows and crossbow quarrels against armour. There is general agreement that the longbow and crossbow led wealthier warriors to discard chain mail in favour of plate in the late 14th and early 15th centuries, but how much more protection did plate armour give?

Vnd also lag menglich mit den panern und
macht wider die von Zürich, und was ein wider
wilen und brant man etwann ein huss oder
zwey und namen ouch was si funden. Und
kament ouch etwann schiff von Zürich mit büchsen und
armbresten und fůren uff dem sewe gegen rüschliken und
schussen zů denen von Lutzern, die hatten ouch ir gůten
tarrass und hantbüchsen bi inen und bruchten die ouch
vast und erschussen in einem schiff einen, darab die von
Zürich vast erschracken, als dick ouch die von Zürich zů
inen schussen als dick ward inen ein huss verbrant, das
macht das si von dem schiessen stůnden.

OPPOSITE
In this curious image the two arquebusiers appear to have weapons with the serpentine locks on opposite sides. Artistic licence or an early accommodation to lefties? From the Swiss *Amtliche Berner Chronik* of 1483, by Diebold Schilling. (Burgerbibliothek Bern, Mss.h.h.I.1, p.141)

Scholars once assumed that longbows were the death of chivalry, slaughtering the flower of French knighthood at battles such as Agincourt in 1415. But this idea raises two further questions – why did plate armour continue to be used throughout the 15th century and well into the 16th century, and why didn't other countries immediately train up large numbers of longbowmen like the English did? Some historians contend that the longbow did not have the penetrative power to punch through plate most of the time, although it did have a severe hampering effect on groups of armoured men and encouraged knights to dismount in battle in order to avoid the loss of their vulnerable and expensive warhorses; even the best *barding* (horse armour) left portions of the horse exposed.

Several different experiments using longbows against various thicknesses of steel at various angles have led to controversial results. Some tests indicate that arrows could not penetrate steel armour; other tests suggest they could at least some of the time. Much ink has been spilt debating the veracity of these different experiments, arguing about the draw and weight of the bows used, the types of arrowheads, the types of steel used for the targets and many other factors. What the sum total of these tests shows is that the penetrative effect of a longbow arrow is a debatable point. In the opinion of this author, it appears a rain of longbow arrows would be more distracting and debilitating than deadly, although there would be the occasional casualty due to lucky shots hitting weak points of the armour or less protected spots such as eyeslits or joints. With the number of arrows blackening the air during a classic English archery storm, the number of lucky shots could have been significant indeed. Eyewitness accounts from Agincourt explicitly state that many French were killed or injured by arrows, but how many? What percentage of arrows that hit an armoured man hurt him by penetrating his defences?

Although unanswerable, an argument can be made through negative evidence. Medieval soldiers did *not* discard their plate, and English-style longbowmen did *not* become universal in medieval warfare. Therefore

Overleaf
This series of photos shows a firing sequence using a button-lock arquebus from the 1470s. This reconstructed arquebus has a bronze barrel and a .62 calibre. It is based on several early images, including a Flemish image from 1473, and was made by John Buck of Musketmart. The re-enactor wears period dress including a reconstruction of the Tongres breastplate, known to be of Flemish manufacture from before 1468 and bearing the town mark of Liège.
This photo sequence had to be reshot to capture the actual firing of the arquebus. During the first photoshoot it was snowing and a snowflake landed right in the pan after it was primed. This turned the priming and some powder granules in the vent into mush, which took a thorough cleaning to clear out. While this was annoying to the re-enactor, it perfectly illustrates one of the many reasons to campaign in the summer. In the next photoshoot the arquebus hang-fired. This was not uncommon and one of the reasons matchlocks replaced button-locks was that if ignition was not immediate, the soldier could try again by simply manipulating the trigger again.
This photoshoot is courtesy of the Company of the Wolfe Argent, a group in the United States that re-enacts soldiers from the army of Charles the Bold, Duke of Burgundy. Bob Reed organized the photoshoot, photos are by Jennifer L. R. Reed, and the re-enactor is Pieter Laubscher, who shortly after these photos were taken went to serve with 3rd Battalion, 172nd Infantry Regiment (Mountain) in Afghanistan.

Hie zwischen warent die von Glarus mit ir paner in das Gastel gezogen / da wartetent si dero von Switz / von etwas anslags wegen der aber wider wegen bleip / durch grosser warnung willen die inen kam das si uber ein mit widerstan solte

Und warent aber die andern eidgnon da zwischent Glarus, lutzern ure und underwalden / Zu denen von zug gezogen und lagent zu Baar mit macht

Und lagent die von zug an ir letzinen mit namen zu baren waag gegen den vienden die an der letze am hirtzel und anderen enden warent und wider wilen mit einandern scharmutzten als man dann tut

Das der lantvogt und die von zurich mit gantzer macht uff dem albis lagent

FIRING AN ARQUEBUS

1. Priming the pan with a small amount of gunpowder. Note the powder horn, satchel for holding shot, and the excess slow match coiled around the stock of the weapon.
2. Close-up of primed pan. Note the pan cover that could swivel over the pan to protect the powder from wind and rain. Generally the lit slow match would be kept well away from the pan during priming, and attached to the 'dog', as seen here, only when the soldier was ready to fire.
3. The handgonner blows lightly on the pan to get rid of excess powder that could flare up at his hands and face, as well as foul the piece more than necessary.
4. Taking the shot from the shot bag. This photo also gives a clear profile view of the arquebus.
5. A close-up of the ball. Modern re-enactors tend to use stainless steel balls rather than the lead balls used by the original handgonners.

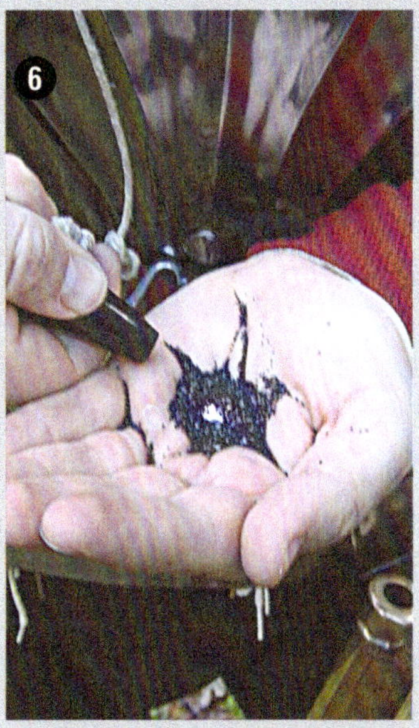

6. A close-up of the measured charge. Some troops were already using pre-measured cartridges by this time, but any soldier worth his salt could quickly measure out a proper charge.

7. Pouring the charge into the barrel.

8. Tamping down the charge.

9. Ramming the ball down the barrel. By this time many handgonnes had a slot beneath the barrel for the ramrod. This practice later became universal.

10. The soldier blows on the slow match to kindle the flame and assure a quick ignition of the priming powder.

11. Presenting the weapon. Note that the soldier doesn't bring his eye close to the barrel in order to aim like with a modern weapon. There is too much danger of eye injury from flare from the priming pan.

12. Firing the weapon.

1

2

3

4

5

6

the longbow was not the revolutionary weapon historians once thought it was. Fewer tests have been performed on crossbows, and it would be interesting to understand why some armies, particularly the French, favoured this weapon.

The important consideration remains of why the handgonne, surely slower and less accurate than the bow or crossbow, would have been developed and retained at all, counting for an ever-increasing percentage of the long-range arsenal of all European armies. The weapon obviously had some practical use that bows and crossbows did not. While the abilities of individual commanders may vary, soldiers tend to be practical and do not retain weapons that prove unreliable in stopping the enemy. So how powerful were early handgonnes?

In the early 1970s, Alan R. Williams of the University of Manchester Institute of Science and Technology test-fired three different replica handgonnes. All had a bore of ¾in (19mm), and varying lengths of 5in (127mm), 10in (254mm) and 15in (381mm). This progression came from an assumed lengthening of barrels over time based on a small sample size of handgonnes, with the 5-inch handgonne supposedly common in the 14th century, the 10-inch in the early 15th century and the 15-inch in the late 15th century.

Test firings used gunpowder of six parts saltpetre, two parts charcoal, and one part sulphur, following the recipe given in the late 13th century text *De Mirabilibus Mundi*. Separate firings were conducted with dry-mixed and wet-mixed powder, firing both lead and steel balls against a 2.54mm mild steel plate at 9.1m.

Results with dry-mixed powder were disappointing. One shot in four misfired, with the powder burning too slowly and thus sending too much gas pressure through the touch-hole. This resulted in the ball having little force, at times simply rolling out of the end of the barrel. It is likely that medieval handgonners were better at making and loading their weapons, but misfires may have been a serious problem. Muzzle velocity for lead balls ranged from 195.1m/s for the short barrel, 152.4m/s for the medium, and 563.9m/s for the long. The results for steel balls were 103.6m/s for the short barrel, 219.5m/s for the medium, and 265.2m/s for the long, but there is no evidence that 15th-century handgonners ever used steel balls.

The wet-mixed powder proved more reliable, with misfires happening less than ten per cent of the time. The powder burned much faster and muzzle velocity increased. The short barrel had a muzzle velocity of 179.8m/s, the medium 158.5m/s, and the long 469.4m/s for lead balls. The results for steel balls were 182.9m/s for the short barrel, 268.2m/s for the medium, and 283.5m/s for the long. In all cases the muzzle velocity of lead balls varied widely, possibly due to irregularities in their shape. Williams found that the handgonnes were generally accurate at 9.1m, but their accuracy became uncertain at longer ranges.

This study, although flawed in many ways and making many assumptions, suggests that handgonne power increased over time. The 15-inch 'late 15th-century' handgonne had more than 50 per cent greater muzzle velocity than the 5-inch '14th-century' handgonne. Furthermore,

1. A hackbut with octagonal barrel from Croatia, dated by the museum to the early 16th century but probably earlier. It is equipped with front and rear sights and four holes on the bottom that appear to have been used for a cord. Perhaps one held the match and the others formed some sort of strap for carrying? Length 1,225mm, calibre 25mm, weight 9.2kg. (Croatian History Museum)

2. Another Croatian hackbut very similar to **1**. Note the simple touch-hole on the side. Dated by the museum to the early 16th century but probably earlier. Length 1,060mm, calibre 20mm, weight 8.2kg. (Croatian History Museum)

3. The butt end of **2**, seen from above. The groove probably held the match as it is very close to the touch-hole. (Croatian History Museum)

4. A very crude Croatian version of a hackbut with the hook clamped onto the hexagonal barrel. Dated by the museum to the early 16th century but probably earlier. Length 1,350mm, calibre 22mm, weight 10.7kg. (Croatian History Museum)

5. Hackbut with octagonal barrel very similar to **1** and **2**. While all three of these Croatian handgonnes are remarkably alike in form, they vary in length and calibre. Dated by the museum to the early 16th century but probably earlier. Length 1,335mm, calibre 23mm, weight 10.9kg. (Croatian History Museum)

6. The butt end of **5**, seen from above. It is almost identical with the butt end of **2**. (Croatian History Museum)

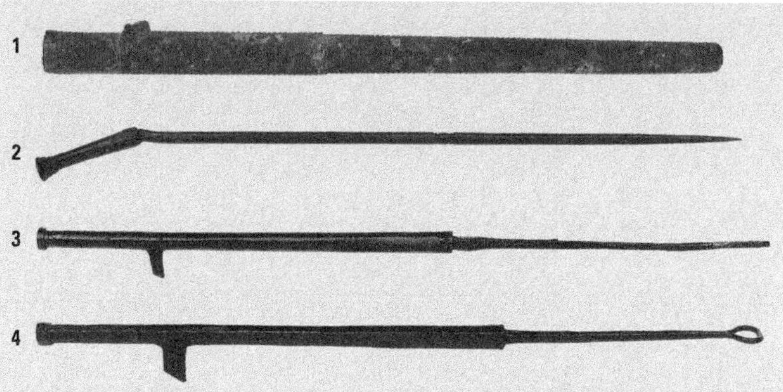

1. Chinese bronze handgonne from the 14th or 15th century. Sea salvage found in the Molucca Sea in the Dutch East Indies. In basic design it is very similar to handgonnes of the same period found half a world away. Note the primitive touch-hole. Length 533mm. One end flared for insertion into pole. Weight approximately 2.3kg. (Photo courtesy David Gonzales, Wisma Antik)
2. This unusual handgonne from the Low Countries has a short barrel and a long, spiked tiller. The tiller may be a later reconstruction, with the socketed barrel originally affixed to a straight wooden stock. (Legermuseum, Delft)
3. Hackbut, 15th century, from the Low Countries. (Legermuseum, Delft)
4. Hackbut, 15th century, from the Low Countries. This example has a horizontal loop at the end of the tiller and a tiny button sight on top of the muzzle. (Legermuseum, Delft)

the 5-inch handgonne failed to penetrate the steel in all of its five hits. The 10-inch handgonne (supposedly representing an early 15th-century model) penetrated six times out of 14 hits, while the 15-inch handgonne penetrated five times out of eight. Penetration with approximately half the hits is better than even the most optimistic estimates of the effectiveness of the longbow.

An incidental observation was that ramming the wadding and powder proved very difficult unless the gonner set the stock rigidly on the ground, suggesting one reason for the long stocks found in most handgonnes.

There has been only one experiment using actual period handgonnes, but the weapons dated from the matchlock period. In 1988 and 1989 the staff at the Landeszeughaus (provincial armoury) in Graz, Austria, fired 14 weapons dating from 1571 to the late 1700s, with roughly equal numbers of weapons from the 16th, 17th and 18th century. Three were rifles and the rest smoothbore muskets. A total of 325 shots were fired using modern hunter's black powder of 0.3–0.6mm grain. The size of the charge equalled one-third of the ball weight.

The team tested only four firearms from the 16th century, the period most relevant to this book: a heavy or 'Spanish' musket called a *Doppelhaken* dating from 1571 (rifled wheel-lock, calibre 19.8mm), another Doppelhaken from the 1580s (wheel-lock and matchlock, calibre 20.6mm), a wheel-lock musket from *c.*1595 (cal. 17.2mm), and a wheel-lock musket from 1593 (cal. 12.3mm). These had respective average muzzle velocities of 482, 533, 456, and 427m/s. Velocity tapered off

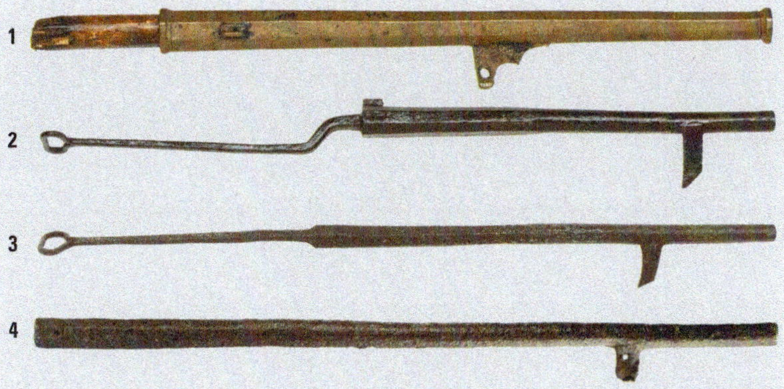

1. Hackbut, 15th century, from the Low Countries. This bronze example has a touch-hole and pan on the side and a socket for a wooden tiller. (Legermuseum, Delft)
2. Hackbut, 15th century, from the Low Countries. The barrel is round on the front two-thirds before becoming octagonal, and appears to have been shortened at some time in the past. The firing pan is on the right-hand side and is fitted with a small button, probably for a swinging pan cover that is now lost. On top of the barrel just above the pan is a rectangular construction with a longitudinal hole, either for sighting or for holding a match. Length 1,335mm, calibre 21mm, weight 10.2kg. (Legermuseum, Delft)
3. Hackbut, late 15th century, from the Low Countries. Wrought iron with welded hook and tiller. The barrel is hexagonal in the rear half and circular in the front half. The oval loop at the end of the tiller is horizontal. The bore is roughly done and not even centred, one side of the barrel being noticeably thinner than the other. Length 1,626mm, barrel 1,020mm, hook 96mm, calibre approximately 27mm. (Legermuseum, Delft)
4. Danish hook gun, *c.*1480, found on the beach on the island of Anholt. This large, crude piece has a touch-hole in the side but, unlike many Danish examples, no sights. Length 1,138mm, calibre 22mm, weight 9.22kg. (Danish National Museum of Military History)

quickly, however, as air resistance was heightened by imperfections in the lead balls. At 100m their velocities had gone down to 305, 349, 287, and 238m/s. Spheres have poor aerodynamics, and the slight irregularities of a lead ball exacerbates this.

The firearms showed impressive penetrative ability. The calibre 19.8mm Doppelhaken pierced 2mm mild steel at 100m. The calibre 20.6 Doppelhaken pierced 4mm steel, the larger wheel-lock pierced 2mm steel, while the smaller wheel-lock pierced only 1mm of steel at the same range. Considering that a suit of armour would rarely be more than 3mm thick at its strongest point, and often half that thickness, the tests suggest that by the late 16th century, black powder weapons could kill a knight at short range.

One shot raised some questions, however. The experimenters fired a wheel-lock pistol from *c.*1620 with a calibre of 12.3mm and a muzzle velocity of 438m/s, at a piece of barding – a breastplate from a horse – made *c.*1575. This was made of 2.8–3mm cold-worked mild steel, and mounted on a sandbag covered with two layers of linen to simulate a

The Battle of Pavia by Ruprecht Heller, (© Nationalmuseum, Stockholm, Sweden/The Bridgeman Art Library)

Cerignola and Pavia: the matchlock proves its worth

The matchlock was the culmination of two centuries of handgonne development. By the beginning of the 16th century, advances in metallurgy, gunpowder production, and battlefield tactics had created a weapon that could take an equal place among older favourites such as armoured cavalry and infantry pike formations.

By this time the old term 'arquebus', originally used for some pre-matchlock handgonnes, had come into common use for matchlocks. Larger specimens were sometimes called 'muskets' – the term which would become common with the next generation of longarms.

The matchlock had a trigger that released a spring-mounted sear, which dropped the match holder into the priming pan, igniting the priming and the main charge. A button-lock mechanism could also be used. Larger examples were steadied on a forked staff stuck into the ground.

Although it was effective, the matchlock's rate of fire was slow. Humfrey Barwick, writing in the late 16th century, said an arquebus took 40 seconds to load and fire, and that it had an effective range of 240 yards when fired in volley. He himself could hit a standing man at 120 yards. Other writers claimed a shorter effective range and slower rate of fire, but all agreed that one had to be at close range to pierce armour. However, although it remained slower than the bow, the Graz Armoury tests (detailed on page 70) show that the arquebus had a greatly superior muzzle velocity, and thus penetrative capability, than a bow, crossbow, or early handgonne.

Two 16th-century battles in particular established the matchlock's reputation as a weapon that could be critical to an army's victory or defeat. In 1503, the French and the Spanish were fighting for control of southern Italy, and on 28 April the Spanish army under Gran Capitán Gonzalo de Córdoba clashed with the French army of Louis d'Armagnac, Duke of Nemours, at Cerignola. The Spaniards chose to defend a slope in a vineyard, which they augmented with a ditch and earthwork; the ditch strengthened by sharpened stakes. Gonzalo lined his arquebusiers, pikemen, and his small number of cannon behind these defences and awaited the French advance.

The French rashly decided to attack without scouting the Spanish position. They sent in their armoured cavalry, which got stopped short by the ditch and gunned down by the arquebusiers. The Duke of Nemours was among those slain. A second wave, composed of Swiss mercenary pikemen, came under heavy fire as they tried to cross the ditch and earthwork. A Spanish counterattack of infantry carrying swords and bucklers (small shields) rushed into the broken lines and slaughtered the Swiss, whose pikes were useless at such close quarters. The survivors fled in disorder and the Spanish captured their artillery train and much of their baggage. Gonzalo's wise use of terrain to maximize the effectiveness of his arquebusiers won the day. The slaughter at Cerignola left at least 3,000 dead on the French side, while the Spaniards suffered barely a hundred casualties.

In 1525, another battle for control of Italy cemented the arquebus's reputation. This time the clash occurred between the French army of King Francis I and the army of Charles V, whose Hapsburg Empire included Spain, Austria, and parts of Germany. Francis led his army in the field, but the Imperial army was commanded by Charles de Lannoy. Both sides used Swiss, German, and Italian mercenaries. The French relied on heavily armoured cavalry, including many nobles, to charge the enemy with lances and then fight with swords in hand-to-hand combat. The French considered their infantry to be of inferior quality, and while they hired many skilled mercenary infantry who employed pikes and arquebuses, the focus was on the heavy cavalry.

The Imperial army was more modern. Its cavalry wasn't as heavily armed and armoured as the French and its commanders mostly relied on infantry. The Spanish infantry consisted of pikemen, arquebusiers, and sword-and-buckler men at a ratio of 2:2:1 – a much higher proportion of arquebusiers than the Swiss or German mercenaries used. Most Swiss infantry were pikemen, with arquebusiers comprising 10 per cent or less. German *Landsknecht* mercenaries were mostly pikemen, supported by swordsmen, halberdiers, and arquebusiers, with the latter comprising 10 per cent or more of the force.

Francis led the French army into northern Italy in late 1524. The smaller Imperial army withdrew into the fortified city of Pavia, which the French then surrounded and put under siege. Pavia had stout defences, plus a river to the south, and a large park surrounded by a wall to the north. The French took the park but found their forces separated, with detachments on the south bank of the river as well as on the north bank to the west and east of town. Two more French forces guarded the walled park to the north. Apart from the two forces inside the park, none of the French detachments could easily come to the aid of another. This was to prove a fatal problem.

An Imperial relief army arrived on 3 February 1525 and set up earthworks to the east of Pavia and the walled park. Three weeks of artillery exchanges and skirmishing followed until, on 24 February, the Imperial army snuck to the north of the park under cover of darkness and breached the wall. Their intention was to defeat the French inside, capture King Francis, and bring much-needed supplies to Pavia.

By the time the French responded, much of the Imperial army had already marched inside. The Imperial forces came between the two French detachments, dividing them into two numerically inferior parts. Francis led his heavy cavalry in a charge, brushing away the lighter Imperial cavalry before coming up against a strong force of Spanish and *Landsknecht* infantry. A disproportionate number of them were arquebusiers, since they had been the first to come through the breach. The French cavalry were soon flanked on both sides. The ground was soft, hampering movement, and a forest in front of them stopped their advance. As the knights became increasingly pressed together and disordered, the Imperial arquebusiers fired on them at close range, punching through their armour while German halberdiers pulled other knights off their horses. The French nobility were slaughtered and King Francis himself was captured. The rest of the French army fled in disorder.

At both Cerignola and Pavia the arquebusiers defeated an enemy limited in their movements by terrain, thus providing ideal targets. It wasn't until the widespread adoption of the flintlock in the 17th century that infantry could stand on the battlefield with black powder weapons alone – without protective shields of pike formations or fortifications – but Cerignola and Pavia certainly proved it to be a winning weapon on the 16th-century battlefield.

ABOVE In this detail of *The Siege of Alesia*, a 1533 painting by Melchior Feselen, we see soldiers firing arquebuses by the matchlock method and by hand. The arquebusier in the centre has his match coiled around a short stick or rod, and clearly does not have a lock on his arquebus. Even at this late date not all guns were fitted with locks. (Alte Pinakothek, Munich, Germany/Giraudon/The Bridgeman Art Library)

clothed man. When the pistol was fired at 8.5m, the ball pierced the armour but failed to pierce even the linen underneath. It had been so deformed by passing through the armour that it had lost virtually all its kinetic energy. The person (or horse) underneath the armour would have suffered only a serious bruise and a nervous moment.

It appears that even in the 16th century, black powder weapons could hope to kill an armoured target only at relatively close range. Considering their poor accuracy, it makes sense that handgonners would assemble in large groups, so an increased number of shots would help ensure enemy casualties.

In 1998, Thom Richardson of the Royal Armouries and his team conducted ballistic tests on a variety of weapons, measuring the velocity of shot from everything from slings to arquebuses. The least effective longbow, with a 72lb draw at 28in (711mm), drawn to 27in (686mm), and firing swallowtail arrows, had an average velocity of 37.4m/s. The most effective longbow, a replica of a specimen found in the *Mary Rose* with a 90lb draw at 28in, drawn to 27in, and firing an arrow also reconstructed from a *Mary Rose* find, had an average velocity of 44.5m/s. The best crossbow tested, a replica of a 15th-century crossbow with a steel bow and a draw weight of 440lb, spanned by a windlass, had an average velocity of 44.7m/s.

Next the team tested a replica 15th-century hackbut firing a 15.75mm lead ball and using a 50-grain charge of modern gunpowder. This had the astonishing average velocity of 180.5m/s, more than four times that of the best crossbow or longbow. Replicas of early 16th-century matchlock arquebuses proved to be even better, with the best having an average velocity of 521.2m/s, firing a 12.7mm lead ball with a 90-grain charge of modern black powder. These results appear to bear out Williams' earlier experiments.

While there are some flaws to these tests, the most glaring being the use of modern powder, the massive superiority of the hackbut and arquebus suggests why these weapons grew in favour – even if medieval powder was only half as good as modern powder, the weapons would have still been more than twice as effective at short ranges as longbows and crossbows.

The point about range is a significant one. Longbows and crossbows had much greater effective ranges than a lead ball, both in terms of accuracy and maintained velocity, and this suggests why they remained in use for such a long time. The mixtures of bowmen and handgonners seen so often in medieval art and chronicles had a purpose; the strengths of one weapon compensated for the weaknesses of the other. After being battered by a hail of arrows, the enemy would draw close enough to receive a salvo of deadly handgonne shot. The knowledge of what they could expect may very well have dissuaded some of the less hearty in the ranks from closing with the archers and handgonners at all. In a later period there is explicit evidence that commanders saw the advantage of mixing weapons. The *Captain's Handbook*, written by Henry Barrett in 1562, recommends using archers and arquebusiers together to keep up a constant fire.

OPPOSITE
Men attacking the Citadel of Women. This Flemish manuscript illustration dates from 1442 or 1443 but shows simple socketed handgonnes still in use. (Champion des Dames by Martin le Franc, Bib. Royale, Ms. 9466, f. 4r, Brussels)

Lack of accuracy seems to have been the handgonne's main weakness besides slow rate of fire. All of the weapons in the Graz tests had poor accuracy, but re-enactors using replica handgonnes have shown that these disadvantages may not have been as great as generally assumed. Hitting man-sized targets at 10m or even 45m with a pre-matchlock handgonne is not impossible, although it does require considerable practice. Hitting a horseman or a group of men would be significantly easier.

During the campaign to relieve the English siege of Orleans in 1429, the French had in their ranks a famous gonner named Master Jean le Cannonier who used a couleuvrine to great effect. A couleuvrine could be either a small cannon or large handgonne. Despite Master Jean's name this couleuvrine was most likely a handgonne because he specialized in picking off individual Englishmen. In one instance he was ordered to shoot down a particularly large and well-armed Englishman who was causing trouble in a fight and did so with no apparent trouble. When he went with Joan of Arc's army to retake the castles on the Loire, Master Jean shot several of the best English defenders off the walls. It is difficult to imagine that Master Jean used an artillery piece, as there is no evidence in this period of any carriage or mounting that would have been sufficiently manoeuvrable to aim at an individual.

Shooting at individuals is possible with a handgonne, but no handgonne could achieve the accuracy of a bow or crossbow at anything other than close range. It must be remembered, however, that accuracy was not as essential in medieval warfare as it is in modern warfare. The handgonner did not generally fire at individuals, but rather at slow-moving masses of men. As long as he did not fire too high or low, he was almost certain to hit somebody. And with his shot more likely than not to cause a casualty, he made an important addition to the ranks of archers and crossbowmen.

So it appears the handgonne was a viable weapon from the beginning, and one that became all the more effective as gunpowder and the weapon's design improved in quality. Only the earliest pieces would have resembled the stereotypically dangerous hand cannon, and even these had a distinct use in the field – that of psychological advantage. In the first half of the 14th century handgonnes, indeed all black powder weapons, were still relatively rare, and setting one off would scare horses and intimidate men. This effect wore off quickly as the technology spread and armies became more accustomed to the smoke, smell, and noise of black powder weapons. By this time, however, handgonnes had become accurate enough to inflict real damage to the enemy.

This must have had a depressing effect on morale, especially for those of the knightly class who realized their armour was vulnerable to some commoner's handgonne. It would be interesting to test the blunt trauma damage caused to a man in armour hit by a handgonne shot that did not penetrate the armour. He would almost certainly have been knocked down, perhaps severely bruised or even have suffered internal haemorrhaging. The knowledge that, unlike an arrow, any sort of hit was going to hurt, must certainly have played upon the mind of anyone facing a handgonner.

GLOSSARY

Terminology was vague in the medieval and early modern period. The same word was often used to refer to widely different objects. Thus the definitions below should be taken only as guidelines to the most common meaning of the word.

arquebus	Small-calibre long gun with shoulder stock. Lit by hand, or with a matchlock, button-lock or wheel-lock mechanism
barding	Horse armour
bombard	Early, forged-iron cannon
bombardelle	Small, portable bombard. Also one of the many early terms for handgonne
bössor	Scandinavian term for a type of small cannon
button-lock	A hand-held black powder weapon fired by pressing a button, which released the match holder onto the priming powder
caltrops	Spiked iron balls
couleuvrine	A small cannon
couleuvrine à main	One of many early terms for a handgonne
cranequin	Portable device for bending a crossbow
culverin	A small cannon
dog	A match holder
Doppelhaken	Heavy musket
fire arrow	Arrow with a small pouch containing gunpowder
fire lance/fire tube	Early gunpowder weapon made of wood, iron, or sheet copper tube
gorgerin	Armour protecting the throat and neck and made of mail or plate
hackbut/haquebut	handgonne with hook for bracing
halberd	Tall spear with an axe blade and spike mounted on the end of the shaft
hook gun	Large handgonne with a form similar to both a hackbut and an arquebus
matchlock	A hand-held black powder weapon fired by pulling a trigger, which released the match holder onto the priming powder. The earliest examples had a simple lever instead of a lock mechanism
pavise/pavisier	Large shield / shield bearer
pistola	Spiked iron balls
pot de fer	Primitive cannon, made of iron
ribalds/ribaudiaux	Wheelbarrows mounted with three or more small cannons with spikes on the front
ruchnitsa	Russian long-barrelled musket handgonne
sallet	Light medieval helmet
samopal	Small type of Russian handgonne
schiopetto	One of many early terms for a handgonne
swivel gun	A large handgonne mounted on a swivel. Used on ships
tyufyak/tyufyaki	Heavy Russian handgonne
vasi	Italian primitive cannon, made of iron
veuglaire	A medium-sized cannon
wheel-lock	A hand-held black powder weapon fired by pressing a trigger, which spun a toothed steel wheel against iron pyrite, sending sparks onto the priming powder

BIBLIOGRAPHY

Books

Boeheim, W., *Handbuch der Waffenkunde*, Nachdruck der Akademischen Druck-und Verlagsanstalt, Graz, Austria (1890)

Brackenbury, Sir Henry, 'Ancient Cannon in Europe' in *Proceedings of the Royal Artillery Institution of Woolwich*, Vols 1 & 2 (1865 & 1866)

Buchanan, Brenda, ed., *Gunpowder: The History of an International Technology*, Bath University Press, Bath (1996)

Burley, Peter, Elliott, Michael, and Watson, Harvey, *The Battles of St. Albans*, Pen & Sword Military, Barnsley (2007)

Crozier, Ronald D., *Guns, Gunpowder and Saltpetre: A Short History*, Faversham Society, Faversham (1998)

Davies, Jonathan, *Gunpowder Artillery 1267–1603: The Development and Employment of Artillery in Britain and Europe*, Stuart Press, Bristol (2003)

Davies, Jonathan, *Guns and Gunpowder 1267–1603*, Stuart Press, Bristol

DeVries, Kelly, 'Gunpowder and Early Gunpowder Weapons' in *Gunpowder: The History of an International Technology*, ed. Brenda Buchanan, Bath University Press (1996)

DeVries, Kelly, *Guns and Men in Medieval Europe 1200–1500*, Ashgate Publishing, Aldershot (2002)

DeVries, Kelly, *Medieval Military Technology*, Broadview Press Ltd, Peterborough, Ont. (1992)

DeVries, Kelly, 'Gunpowder Weapons at the Siege of Constantinople' in *War and Society in the Eastern Mediterranean, 7th–15th Centuries*, Brill Academic Publishers, Leiden (1996)

Gravett, Christopher, *Tewkesbury 1471*, Osprey Publishing, Oxford (2003)

Hale, J. R., *War and Society in Renaissance Europe 1450–1620*, Sutton Publishing, Stroud (1998)

Hall, Bert, 'The Corning of Gunpowder and the Development of Firearms in the Renaissance' in *Gunpowder: The History of an International Technology*, ed. Brenda Buchanan, Bath University Press (1996)

Hall, Bert, *Weapons and Warfare in Renaissance Europe*, The Johns Hopkins University Press, London (2001)

Heath, Ian, *Byzantine Armies AD 1118–1461*, Osprey Publishing, Oxford (1995)

Hogg, O. F. G., *Artillery: Its Origin, Heyday, and Decline*, C. Hurst & Co (1970)

Hogg, O. F. G., *English Artillery 1326–1716*, Royal Artillery Institution, London (1963)

Kempers, R. T. W., 'Haquebuts from Dutch Collections' in *Journal of the Arms and Armour Society*, Vol. 11, No. 2 (December 1983), pp.56–89

Krenn, Peter, Kalaus, Paul, and Hall, Bert, 'Material Culture and Military

History: Test-Firing Early Modern Small Arms' in *Material History Review* 42 (1995), pp.101–109

Miller, Douglas, and Embleton, Gerry, *The Swiss at War 1300–1500*, Osprey Publishing, Oxford (1998)

Nicolle, David, *Constantinople 1453: The End of Byzantium*, Osprey Publishing, Oxford (2000)

Nicolle, David, *Italian Medieval Armies 1300–1500*, Osprey Publishing, Oxford (1983)

Norris, John, *Early Gunpowder Artillery c.1300–1600*, Crowood Press, Ramsbury (2003)

Partington, J. P., *A History of Greek Fire and Gunpowder*, The Johns Hopkins University Press, Baltimore (1999)

Patrick, John Merton, *Artillery and Warfare During the 13th and 14th Centuries*, Utah State University Press, Salt Lake City (1961)

Petrovi , Djurdjica, 'Fire-arms in the Balkans on the Eve of and after the Ottoman Conquest of the Fourteenth and Fifteenth Centuries' in *War, Technology and Society in the Middle East*, Oxford University Press, London (1975)

Phillips, Gervase, 'Longbow and Hackbut: Weapons Technology and Technology Transfer in Early Modern England' in *Technology and Culture*, Vol. 40, No. 3 (July 1999), pp.576–593

Richardson, Thom, 'Ballistic Testing of Historical Weapons' in *Royal Armouries Yearbook* 3 (1998), pp.50–52

Rimer, Graeme, 'Early Handguns' in *Royal Armouries Yearbook* 1 (1996), pp.73–78

Rogers, Clifford, 'The Military Revolutions of the Hundred Years' War' in *The Journal of Military History*, Vol. 57, No. 2 (April 1993), pp.241–278

Smith, Robert D., 'The Reconstruction and Firing Trials of a Replica of a 14th-century Cannon' in *Royal Armouries Yearbook* 4 (1999), pp.86–94

Tittmann, Wilfried, 'The Guns of Archbishop Baldwin of Trier 1331/32 and the Guns in the Milemete Manuscripts of 1326/27: Some Critical Comments' in *Journal of the Ordnance Society* 17 (2005), pp.5–23

Tout, T. F., 'Firearms in England in the Fourteenth Century' in *The English Historical Review*, Vol. 26, No. 104 (October 1911), pp.666–702

Turnbull, Stephen, *The Hussite Wars 1419–36*, Osprey Publishing, Oxford (2004)

Van Den Brink, Jan M., 'A Late Medieval Hackbut' in *Journal of the Arms and Armour Society*, Vol. 6, No. 9 (March 1970), pp.241–43

Williams, Alan R., 'Some Firing Tests with Simulated Fifteenth-Century Handguns' in *Journal of the Arms and Armour Society*, Vol. 8 (1974–76), pp.114–120

Websites

Medieval Gunpowder Research Group, Reports No. 1, 2, 3, 4 & 8, from www.middelaldercentret.dk, retrieved 15 September 2009

INDEX

Figures in **bold** refer to illustrations.